1998

Making Sense of Managing Culture

Making Sense of Managing Culture

David Cray and Geoff Mallory

INTERNATIONAL THOMSON BUSINESS PRESS
I(T)P® An International Thomson Publishing Company

London • Bonn • Boston • Johannesburg • Madrid • Melbourne • Mexico City • New York • Paris
Singapore • Tokyo • Toronto • Albany, NY • Belmont, CA • Cincinnati, OH • Detroit, MI

Making Sense of Managing Culture

Copyright © 1998 David Cray and Geoff Mallory

First published by International Thomson Business Press

I(T)P® A division of International Thomson Publishing Inc.
The ITP logo is a trademark under licence

British Library Cataloguing-in-Publication Data
A catalogue record for this book is available from the British Library

First edition 1998

Typeset by LaserScript Limited, Mitcham, Surrey
Printed in the UK by Clays Ltd, Bungay, Suffolk

ISBN 1 86152 178 2 paperback
ISBN 1 86152 177 4 hardback

International Thomson Business Press   International Thomson Business Press
Berkshire House   20 Park Plaza
168–173 High Holborn   13th Floor
London WC1V 7AA   Boston MA 02116
UK   USA

http:\\www.itbp.com

This book is affectionately dedicated to Sebastian Michael Cray, seasoned world traveller, first baseman extraordinaire and founding member of Saturday Night In.

Contents

List of figures and tables   ix
Preface   xi

1   A larger and smaller world   1
Issues in comparative organizational behaviour   4
The retreat from theory   12
The way forward   20
Selected readings   21

2   Traditional approaches to comparative research   23
Differences and universals   23
The naive comparative approach: compared to what?   29
*Culture-free: an oil refinery is an oil refinery is an oil
    refinery*   37
Culture-bound theories: Hofstede and friends   49
The three traditional approaches in perspective   57
Conclusion   58
Selected readings   60

3   Strategy and culture   63
Introduction   63
Strategy formulation   68
Joint ventures   75
Acquisitions   80
Technology transfer   83
Conclusion: strategy, culture and cognition   85
Selected readings   88

4   Culture and cognition   89
Introduction   89

Cognition in organizations 92
A model of cultural effects on behaviour modified by
  cognition 98
Selected readings 112

5 People and culture 113
  Introduction 113
  International human resource management 115
  Leadership 123
  Transfer of working practices 130
  People, international systems and cognition 135
  Selected readings 136

6 A cognitive approach to international management 139
  The four- (or five-) dimensional cage 139
  Issues for a cognitive theory 144
  Approaches and issues in cognitive research 146
  Building a cognitive theory of comparative organizational
    behaviour 159
  Selected readings 161

  References 163
  Index 179

List of figures and tables

FIGURES

4.1	Example of a cognitive map	96
4.2	Basic cultural model	98
4.3	Individual cognition as an intervening variable	99
4.4	Adding organizational culture to the model	101
4.5	The cognitive model	106
6.1	Sense-making sensitivity in international and domestic contexts	155

TABLES

1.1	Issues in comparative organizational behaviour	12
1.2	Barriers to comparative research	20
2.1	Three traditional approaches to cross-cultural research	25
2.2	Comparative and internationalist approaches	28
2.3	Representative naive comparative studies	36
2.4	Representative culture-free studies	42
2.5	Summary of Donaldson's (1986) findings on size and bureaucracy	45
2.6	Representative studies utilizing Hofstede's dimensions	56
3.1	Approaches to international business strategy and their treatment of culture	67
3.2	Representative studies of the effects of culture on strategy formulation	74
3.3	Representative studies of cultural effects on international joint ventures	80

3.4 Representative studies of cultural effects on mergers and
      acquisitions   84
5.1 Representative studies of the effects of culture on human
      resource management   123
5.2 Representative studies of the effects of culture on
      leadership   129
5.3 Representative studies of cross-cultural transfer of work
      practices   134

Preface

The tremendous growth in international business over the last two decades has seen a parallel explosion in the literature devoted to the problems and techniques of managing across cultural boundaries. As with many explosions, this one has generated a good deal of noise and confusion, along with some heat and light. Since the literature that has been produced stems from contrasting theoretical stances spread across several disciplines, the findings often offer contradictory interpretations and recommendations. This is hardly surprising given the complexity of the field and the diversity of contexts in which research takes place, but such considerations offer small consolation to managers and employees seeking guidance for interactions with colleagues from other cultural backgrounds. For researchers, the richness of the field provides plenty of scope in terms of both issues and methods, but it inhibits the development of the area as studies are seldom comparable or cumulative.

In this book we consider the field of comparative organizational behaviour with two major ends in mind. First, we want to orient the reader to the field as it now stands by investigating three established approaches in terms of their theoretical anchors and by examining the products of these views and their limitations through research into some key issues in international management. Second, we want to suggest a framework, based on cognitive approaches to organizational behaviour, which we feel helps to overcome some of the limitations of current work. We will argue that a cognitive approach provides greater insight into the problems of international management because it helps establish the links between different levels of culture, specifically between national culture and individual behaviour. Most existing literature assumes a direct, unmediated link between the national and individual levels. We believe that the reality of global corporations is considerably more complex and will endeavour to explain some of the implications of that belief.

Our understanding of the problems involved in operating a cross-cultural organization stems from our reading and research but also from our own experience. There is probably no industry in this global era that is more culturally diverse than higher education. Our students and colleagues are drawn from around the world. Our papers are refereed, edited and, occasionally, read by an international audience. The ideas that we seize upon for our work may come from Finland or New Zealand as well as from our own local academic milieu. The competition for students, personnel and resources is increasingly international in scope. Academics, and the institutions in which they work, have necessarily become more attuned to the issues inherent in cross-cultural operations. As a group, those interested in international business tend to be even more involved in cross-cultural activities than their colleagues in other disciplines.

In this the two authors are fairly typical. David Cray was born and raised in the United States, did his PhD research in England and France, has published with colleagues from Poland, the UK, Canada, the US, Australia and Sweden, and for the last fifteen years has taught in Canada, where he recently helped to establish an international business degree programme involving student exchanges to six countries. Geoff Mallory was born in the UK, taught four years in Canada, and as part of his current position at the Open University Business School has supervised courses and training in Ireland, the Netherlands and Singapore. He has served as the British representative on a major European research project which involved investigators from seven countries. Between us we have supervised graduate students from Yemen, Turkey, Spain, Hong Kong, Japan, Eritrea, Ghana, China and France, among other countries. With these experiences it is hardly a wonder that we are interested in how culture affects the way people from diverse societies interact with the world and with their counterparts. The spirit of inquiry that motivated this book is not simply an academic pursuit but an extension of our own attempts to understand the outlooks, arguments and emotions of our colleagues, students and research subjects.

As with most complex endeavours we have been assisted and encouraged by a number of people who acted from no more complicated motive than the desire to see us succeed. If, in the end, we have not reached quite as high as we hoped, it is certainly our deficiencies and not theirs which are at fault. We wish to thank Dave Wilson, an old friend from the Bradford Welders' days, who first suggested that we write this book and who gave us valuable comments on an early draft. Nicolas Papadopoulos in Canada, Marilyn Fenwick and Andrew Seen in Australia, and Kevin Daniels and Tim Clark in the UK provided valuable critiques of various chapters. An anonymous reviewer also provided valuable suggestions on how the structure of the book might be improved. Thanks also goes to Gerry Griffin, Head of the Department of Management at Monash University in Melbourne, and David Asch, the Dean of the Open University Business School, the former for providing a sabbatical haven for production of the final draft, the latter for support and help when the going got tough. We must also acknowledge, briefly but sincerely, the colleagues at Carleton, Monash and the Open Univeristy who gave us encouragement along the way. Richard Schroeder, also from Monash, helped with the technical details. No one contributed more to the readability and clarity of this book than Ellen Nichols Cray, who, as always, managed to combine overall support with a critical editorial stance in effective measure. Her notation 'not a graceful sentence' managed to imply that the writers had momentarily (and unaccountably) departed from the highest standards but that rectification was merely a matter of applying available skills. To the extent that we were able to attain a state of literary grace, it is largely due to her help. She also helped considerably in clarifying the distinctions among various cognitive approaches. Finally, we wish to thank David Hickson and Derek Pugh, whose interest in and attitude toward research into comparative organizational behaviour has done much to shape our own. By coincidence (or maybe not) the two of them were drafting a book (Hickson and Pugh 1995) on the same topic at the time that work commenced on this volume. A reading of the two books will show that the authors hold somewhat different views on the subject. The degree to which these intellectual differences impinged on our social relationship is accurately reflected in the following exchange, which took place between two of the authors when they discovered they were writing on the same topic.

CRAY: What is your book going to say?
HICKSON: We're going to say, 'Hofstede was right.'
CRAY: Well, we're going to say, 'Hofstede was wrong.'
HICKSON: That's all right then.

It is in this spirit of constructive debate that we offer this work and it is in this spirit that we hope it will be read.

1   A larger and smaller world

The world of organizations and managers has expanded dramatically in the last decade. Suppliers, customers, competitors and personnel now move easily across national borders. Developments such as the integration of the European Union (EU), the implementation of the North American Free Trade Agreement (NAFTA), the conclusion of the Uruguay round of the General Agreement on Tariffs and Trade (GATT) and the subsequent establishment of the World Trade Organization (WTO), and the entry into the world economic marketplace of the former Soviet Union and its client states have provided emerging opportunities for the expansion of international operations. The managers and employees of an increasing number of commercial and non-commercial organizations encounter these wider international realities in their strategic and tactical thinking, as well as in their daily activities.

Operating in parallel with the expansion of the international environment has been the continuing revolution in communication technology, which has brought geographically dispersed individuals and groups into closer contact. Research and development projects are carried out with team members several thousand miles apart (Allen and Hauptman 1990). Contract negotiations take place in real time between groups located on separate continents. Multinational firms are able to monitor the performance of their foreign sub-units more closely and to correct deficiencies more quickly. Organizational tasks in the expanding business world can be observed more minutely and coordinated in detail from virtually any place in the world.

These continuing changes have placed new demands on organizations and those who work in them. An increasingly international environment requires that managers be aware of developments around the world (Ghoshal 1987). This implies that new systems of information collection and processing are needed so that decisions can be made quickly and accurately. Internationalization has also meant that staff within the global organization more often work with others of a different culture or whose formative years were spent in another country.

Increasing international activity makes additional demands on the skills of those who participate in cross-cultural activities. They are faced with interpreting the actions and attitudes of individuals and organizations operating in contexts quite different from their own. They must negotiate with groups that have not only different goals but different methods of reaching them and different expectations of their counterparts' behaviour. The expanding diversity of the organizational world, coupled with the accelerating pace of environmental change, places cognitive demands on organizational members who are often ill equipped to handle them.

The field of comparative management or, as we prefer, comparative organizational behaviour, has reacted to the expansion of international organizational activity with an outpouring of observation, research and advice. Although relatively little of this work has found its way into academic journals (Godkin *et al.* 1989; Boyacigiller and Adler 1991), the results of these efforts provide some guidance for those operating in the international context. Studies exist which compare countries around the world in terms of values, specific behaviours or more abstract, composite dimensions (Hofstede 1980a, 1991; Lincoln *et al.* 1986). Descriptions of managerial actions, values and patterns of thought have been elaborated for numerous cultural contexts (Hickson and Pugh 1995). There are discussions of the importance of cultural differences for structure and processes in integrated international firms. Although some of these findings and recommendations are vague and contradictory, they illuminate important differences in organizational behaviour to which those working in an international context should be attentive.

At another level, however, the fields of comparative and international management have not yet begun to meet the challenges raised by the rise of global management (Redding 1994). For the most part the field is still mired in a centrist view of international management. This view, based on the traditional multinational corporate form, regards foreign subsidiaries and suppliers as clients who must be managed from the centre of the organization, corporate headquarters in the home country. The centrist firm imposes control through home-country managers who are temporarily assigned abroad. For an expatriate manager the crucial issues revolve around differences (or similarities) between the home country and the country of assignment. For example, in a negotiation do the locals get right down to business or do they socialize first? Does their initial position represent a genuine offer or a wild exaggeration of what they will accept? The important point from this perspective is for the manager to be able to fit into, or at least engage with, the local culture. If the manager should move to a third country a similar process of cultural discovery and adjustment would be required. All international relationships are seen as binational links between the centre and specific foreign cultures.

As international organizations have evolved in response to global market pressures the centrist view has been overtaken by the demands of international integration. The basic issue that must be addressed in the context of global business is not that of multinational executives sent abroad but that of managers – or, increasingly, employees at lower levels in the organization – who must operate in a multicultural setting wherever they find themselves (Rao and Schmidt 1995). The increased emphasis on information flows and organizational learning, on company-wide teams and internal flexibility, makes the centrist model inadequate and in some instances limiting. The new global reality of organizations means that many in the workforce have contact with those involved in international business; the managers who work abroad are only a small proportion of those concerned. While much of the comparative field is still operating on the model of the British Empire, managers are working in the context of the European Union.

The comparative organizational behaviour field does not yet provide any general perspective on dealing with the increasingly complex international world of organizations. While Redding (1994) maintains that Hofstede's (1980a, 1991) work supplies a partial paradigm, we will argue that his approach is both too narrow and too static for emerging international realities. For reasons that will be discussed below, there is no clear theoretical basis for the field of comparative management and, indeed, rarely any theoretical referent at all. This lack has prevented the findings of existing studies from being integrated into any coherent framework or statement. More importantly, from our point of view, the focus on specific contrasts among managerial processes and organizational structures has led to an incomplete – and, in important ways, limited – view of comparative organizational behaviour (Boyacigiller and Adler 1991). Processes at more basic levels have been neglected in favour of the description of observable differences. The current international context requires studies that illustrate how managers and other employees adapt their cognitive frameworks, their sense-making abilities (Thomas *et al.* 1993; Weick 1995), to cope with a world that is increasingly multinational, multicultural and dynamic. This approach requires a shift away from a descriptive agenda to one which focuses on the way that organizational members deal with the differentiated environment generated by the international context.

In this book we will attack the problem of understanding comparative issues in three steps. First, we will examine the traditional approaches to comparative organizational behaviour, both to glean insights into the types of problems faced by international employees and to understand the methods by which these descriptions were derived. As we will argue in Chapter 2, there is much to be learned from these studies, provided that they are properly interpreted. Second, in Chapters 3 and 5 we will examine a number of specific macro and micro issues in the international field in terms of their implications for an emerging theory of international organizational behaviour. Finally, in Chapters 4 and 6 we will propose some guidelines and examine some techniques that such an approach might utilize. Our purpose is to provide the elements of a new framework for understanding and analysing organizational behaviour across cultural boundaries, and to suggest how they might be integrated into a comprehensive theory of comparative organizational behaviour.

ISSUES IN COMPARATIVE ORGANIZATIONAL BEHAVIOUR

The growth in international activity and the diversity of organizational forms and institutional practices that it has engendered have given rise to a number of issues in the field which are only beginning to be addressed (Redding 1994). Investigation of these problems is driving the field toward a new view of comparative management and away from the centrist point of view. While the underlying dimensions of this approach are still emerging, a major shift appears to be away from a focus on difference and toward an emphasis on intercultural complexity and its effects. This introduces a more systemically based view of comparative organizational behaviour which regards the integration of complex, intercultural organizations as the key research problem. One of the fundamental issues in the field is the response, organizational and individual, to the increased complexity of the international market.

Responses to increased complexity

There has been a great deal of work published in the past few years on international business strategy. Writers and researchers attempt to identify the important factors that organizations must confront in the global environment. Bartlett and Ghoshal (1987), for example, add organizational learning to the usual considerations of global efficiency and local responsiveness. Including this dimension in the strategic framework has two implications. First, it means that managers must acquire a new set of skills to process information from a global network on an ongoing basis. They must also encourage subordinates to generate and transmit that information not only to their superiors but also to other relevant nodes in the organization. It also means that the manager and others in the organization have to be willing to act on the new information – learning does not occur simply by accumulating information from numerous sources.

The second implication stems from the results of organizational learning. One of the consequences of organizational learning is that the context of management is evolving over time. This has always been true, of course, but older models of strategic adaptation saw changes in structure and process as episodic, often triggered by crisis situations. With the new emphasis on organizational learning, complexity takes on an additional temporal dimension. Strategy must not only take into account current developments and anticipate new ones; it must do so from a continually changing base.

While the work of those writing about international strategy has reflected the increasing complexity of the international organization, the comparative organizational behaviour field has not. When confronted with having to glean and incorporate information flows across cultural boundaries, managers and employees need to be aware of the different biases that may occur. For example, in certain cultures there may be a tendency for higher-level managers to restrict the flow of information because this is seen to enhance status or power. A manager seeking to encourage organizational learning may well need guidance on how to deal with this situation. The current literature has very little to offer either in practical terms or in underlying theories which might assist the manager in this task.

The implications of this new type of environmental context can be seen in the case of a Canadian oil firm that wished to invest in a field in the former Soviet Union (Cray 1994). Naturally the firm had standard procedures for evaluating the potential of a possible production site. However, in this case the firm first had to decide whether it should accept the geological and production data of its local partner or conduct its own research. Since the operations of the local partner were in disarray, the reliability of the Russian data was somewhat suspect. Doing its own exploratory drilling would decrease uncertainty but increase the Canadian company's costs and, what was more important in this case, considerably lengthen the time it would take to arrive at an agreement. Later in the decision process another complication arose from the competing jurisdictional claims of three levels of government. None of these issues was unprecedented in the company's overseas history, but the collection of these and numerous other issues placed in an unfamiliar and rapidly changing political context increased the complexity of the decision-making process substantially, both in negotiations with the firm's potential partners and in the firm's internal procedures. The changing relations among the players caused considerable difficulty for the firm and resulted in an intricate set of agreements with all three levels of government.

On the one hand, the response to this added complexity could be seen in the internal legal, financial and operational arrangements the company made to exploit the field. On the other hand, the arrangements were informed by the culture with which the company was dealing. Current materials from the field have very little to say about the interaction of commercial complexity and cultural variation, and even less to say about the dynamics by which the interaction affects strategic decision-making or other organizational behaviours.

Cultural integration

One of the key issues for managers in international organizations is the problem of integrating employees from several cultures. At one level the problem is the familiar one of overcoming value and behavioural differences that arise when employees from different cultures must work together. For example, an organization with its headquarters in a country which gives considerable deference to leaders may encounter difficulties in promulgating its policies in a country in which consultation among supervisors and subordinates is the norm. The literature is replete with studies that detail these differences, but theoretical or applied treatments which would help a manager to deal with the consequences of these differences have been in very short supply. The international manager is admonished to be aware of these differences and to minimize them, but is given precious little advice on how to do so.

As indicated above, the problem of integration is becoming more pressing as organizations become more geographically diverse and culturally complex. The rapid pace of economic change and the need to respond quickly to customers, suppliers and other segments of the organization mean that higher levels of integration are needed, making culturally induced problems more noticeable. When organizations adapt systems to increase integration other complications arise. Consider, for example, a decision-support system which links managers in several countries. If the system is designed in a country where each individual is expected to champion his/her point of view it may well run into difficulties when it includes those from a culture where deference or reticence is the norm. Such group members may simply not participate or may defer to whomever they perceive as the boss. The implications for these types of systems, which are becoming more and more important to the integration of global organizations, are largely unknown (Shore and Venkatachalam 1995). Not even the usual anecdotal evidence has begun to appear.

In addition to the implications for integration through support systems, there is the larger issue of organizational design. One of the outcomes of the emphasis on more flexible organizational structures has been an increasing concern with organization design. The classic trade-off between organizational flexibility and responsiveness becomes more difficult when the need for flexibility increases at the same time as response times are being shortened. How can organizations be designed which will accommodate different levels of tolerance for ambiguity and complexity? How will the need for rapid evolution of the organization's structure be tied to the contrasting time horizons found in different cultures (Hofstede and Bond 1988)? The current literature offers little, if any, direction for the inquiring designer.

Overall, the problem of integration across geographic distance and cultural diversity is one that can be expected to become more prominent and more intricate as organizations grow to reflect the larger number of countries with developed markets. This will be especially true as the volatile economies of the Pacific Rim require more managerial attention. The combination of cultural distance and institutional change will demand creative solutions to problems of organizational integration.

Levels of culture

There are two considerable organizational literatures that focus on the concept of culture. The comparative literature is built on the concept of national culture expressed at the societal level. The literature on corporate culture takes the organization as its unit of analysis. For the most part, the two literatures and the concepts they embody have remained separate. Yet if we look at problems such as cross-cultural integration it is necessary to consider both types of culture and to understand how they interact.

One method of integration that continues to be used in many organizations with diverse workforces is the promotion of a cohesive culture. The advantages of having a uniform, thick culture have been well advertised. However, if national cultures and organizational cultures are both built on the adherence to particular values, then the difficulties that may arise from clashes of the two value systems are easy to imagine. The solution to this problem goes to the heart of international organizational behaviour. To date there has been little systematic investigation into how the two cultures interact. Hofstede and his associates have concluded that the two cultural systems are essentially separate (Hofstede *et al.* 1990). They argue that national culture is derived from early socialization, while the corporate or organizational culture springs from specific organizational practices. National culture may affect organizational culture mainly through the nationality of the founder (Hofstede 1985). According to Hofstede, professional or industrial groupings may also develop distinct cultures which vie with those based on corporation and nation in influencing behaviour.

There are two key questions embedded in this issue. The first is the extent to which one can regard the various levels of culture in an organization as conceptually distinct. If the national values are given primacy – or, to put it another way, if the values acquired in early childhood are linked to the national level – what does that imply for the values that support organizational culture? They become either subsidiary to national cultural values or entirely separate. The answer to this question has important implications for the promotion of a cohesive global culture. If the two levels of culture are regarded as separate the corporate culture need not adapt itself to the local culture; indeed, it may not need to take it into account at all. If the two are linked, then clearly the articulation of a cohesive global culture becomes much more problematic and tortuous. It most likely means that the organizational culture will be thin and superficial, relying heavily on easily manipulable symbols.

If the two (or more) levels of culture can be seen as conceptually distinct what is their connection? This is much more than a theoretical issue. A manager faced with a work team scattered across several countries needs to build a culture that is to some extent common to all participants. At the same time the manager has to be sensitive to the cultural differences that surely exist. If one takes the national culture as given, then what steps can be taken to alter the organizational culture to accommodate diverse values, expectations and working practices? To what degree should the team culture be specific to those involved and to what extent should it reflect the overall culture of the institution? The literature has been remarkably silent on this set of issues despite the burgeoning use of multicultural teams interacting in real time.

Negotiation

An issue in comparative organizational behaviour which has gained importance recently is that of cross-cultural negotiation. Increasing internationalization, especially the decline in barriers to international trade and the rise of globally integrated enterprises, has meant that negotiations with suppliers, customers, regulatory agencies and even other portions of the organization often cross cultural boundaries. All negotiations are heavily influenced by the behaviour of the parties at the table. Since offers and counter-offers depend on evaluations of what the other side means as well as what they say, cross-cultural negotiations provide extra barriers to reaching agreement. Under these circumstances, correctly interpreting and acting upon cultural cues can be crucial (Adler and Graham 1989). The actions of those from another culture are often systematically misinterpreted, to the detriment of both parties (Graham 1985).

The processes and outcomes of international business negotiations are quite complex. Tung (1988) lists five dimensions on which negotiations may be examined: contextual environment, negotiation context, negotiation characteristics, strategy and negotiation outcomes. Each of these dimensions involves several variables, most of which may vary across cultures. For example, the issues that are regarded as legitimate matters for discussion within a negotiation may differ from culture to culture. The process by which agreements are reached and the status of the agreement at the end of the negotiation (indeed the very definition of closure) are often perceived differently in contrasting societies.

An illustration of these differences occurred in the interaction between a delegation of Canadian academics and their Chinese counterparts in negotiations to set up an exchange with an institute in Beijing. The long-term objective of the Canadians' visit was to assist the Chinese institution in setting up a management programme. Since the visit took place shortly after China opened up to such initiatives neither side had much experience in Sino-Canadian negotiations, although individuals on both sides had considerable experience operating outside their own cultures. After two days of the usual introductions, tours and banquets the two sides sat down to negotiate the terms of the deal. The Chinese presented a list of their requirements, and the research and educational opportunities that they thought they could offer in return. Working through the list item by item, the two sides quickly agreed on most of the points. A few proposals had to be referred back to the Canadian principals, but the team agreed to recommend that they be accepted. At the end of the day both sides seemed pleased. They agreed to meet the following morning to go over the text of the agreement and to finalize any outstanding details. When the Chinese presented the list the next morning, however, it was noticeably different from what had been agreed upon the day before. For the items that the Chinese were to provide, such as research opportunities, the levels had been reduced by about 25 per cent. The items that they were to receive, such as graduate placements in Canada, had been increased by a similar amount. On seeing these alterations, the leader of the Canadian team wished to leave Beijing immediately. He felt the Chinese were not to be trusted since they had unilaterally changed the agreement. The Chinese, for their part, were appalled by the obvious anger on the Canadian side and deeply puzzled by this reaction. The negotiations continued for several more days, but the atmosphere had soured, and the feeling of cooperation and accomplishment had evaporated.

The problems between the two delegations stemmed from divergent perceptions of the negotiation process and its outcomes. The Canadians believed at the end of the first day that they had a firm agreement. The Chinese had proposed, the two teams had discussed and both sides accepted the terms. As the Canadians saw it, all that remained was implementation. The Chinese, on the other hand, regarded the first agreement as a set of initial positions from which the real bargaining might begin. Obviously, if the Canadian team were not willing to better the deal they would have argued much more strenuously over its initial terms. The Chinese did not wish to look weak or foolish by agreeing to a deal which could be improved upon.

This type of misperception, and its attendant difficulties, is common in international negotiations. Although cross-national negotiations are receiving more attention in the literature (Graham 1985; Adler and Graham 1989; Weiss 1994), the underlying problems of interpretation are usually lost in descriptions of actual behaviours. The analysis of such negotiations poses important issues for the relationship between the cultures in which the parties are embedded and the cognitive frameworks which they bring to the table. As Tung (1988) points out, there are numerous factors that can influence cross-cultural negotiations. Developing a theory which ties even a small number of them to the effects of culture is clearly a daunting task. Some of these issues, and those related to other issues in comparative organizational behaviour, are summarized in Table 1.1.

Table 1.1 Issues in comparative organizational behaviour

Current issues	Representative topics
Increased complexity	Greater geographical diversity Increased unit interdependence Expanded information flows Organizational learning
Cultural integration	Interaction with multiple cultures Multicultural workforce Cross-cultural interaction throughout the organization
Levels of culture	National or societal Organizational culture Industrial culture Professional culture
Cross-cultural negotiation	Definitions of negotiation Closure Variation in process Interpretation of offers and proposals

THE RETREAT FROM THEORY

Changes in the structure, processes, dynamics and even conceptualization of international organizations have given rise to a
voluminous literature. They have also focused attention on the
implications of these developments for organizations operating
across cultural boundaries. While there has been a spate of books
describing how to conduct business in country A or how to negotiate
with the government in country B, the theoretical response to these
changing conditions has been severely limited. If anything, the new
literature, taken as a whole, represents a retreat from theorizing
about the issues found in international organizational behaviour.

In part, the retreat from theory simply reflects the general
tendency, especially notable in North America, for business – and
hence organizational – literature to become more applied. The
demand for tools to help combat the international competitive
pressures being felt around the world has led to books which end up
on bestseller lists. Such works do not generally emphasize the
theoretical underpinnings, assuming there are any, of the author's
arguments. The irony of all this is that, while much of the

revitalization of interest in organization theory derived from the first manifestations of the current round of global competition, the same interest has helped to drive out any demand for basic theoretical work. Like much current product development the emphasis has been more on marketing and less on the product itself.

The retreat from theory also arises from a basic misunderstanding of the phenomenon, which itself may be due to the existing literature. By far the greatest emphasis in comparative organizational behaviour (as opposed to international management) has been on the differences, the contrasts, the overall diversity of behaviour in different cultures. The literature, both academic and popular, is replete with cautionary tales concerning the disasters that await those who do not understand the deep divisions between cultures. What is missing is any hint that there may be a framework that will allow either the practitioner or the theorist to understand these phenomena in a systematic way (Redding 1994). The impression has been given that such a theoretical base is out of reach – except, perhaps, for limited areas. Indeed, the only cross-national approach that proposes a universal theory, the structurally based culture-free approach (discussed in Chapter 2), does so precisely by arguing that the same forces have equivalent effects in all cultures. No comprehensive theory of comparative organizational behaviour has been proposed, and even the possibility of developing one seems to have been abandoned.

Theoretical difficulties

While the theoretical underdevelopment of international organizational behaviour is part of a larger trend in organizational studies, it also reflects some of the specific difficulties that attach to comparative and cross-national research. These can be gathered under three main headings: theoretical, conceptual and methodological. As mentioned above, the absence of a unifying theory (or even clearly articulated competing theories) of comparative organizational behaviour is a traditional theme of the critics (Boyacigiller and Adler 1991). Anyone who scans a selection of the literature can only agree. Why, then, is there no generally acceptable theory of comparative management?

The first difficulty lies in the variety of the phenomena being studied. Even within purely domestic organizational behaviour there are numerous aspects to be studied. There are managerial functions, industrial relations, conflict, structure, cognitive aspects, and so on. When this type of study is extended to other countries this list increases, since what may be important to organizational theorists and managers in one country may not address what is important elsewhere. There is hardly a unifying theory in organization theory; the complicating factor of culture makes it even more difficult to construct one for comparative organizational behaviour.

The variety of the phenomena to be explained is also reflected in the number of academic disciplines which have examined cross-cultural behaviour. Sociology, psychology, anthropology, political science, business and economics have all generated distinctive literatures and contrasting theoretical stances within which that literature is located. These provide a variety of interpretive glosses for the data collected. As Roberts and Boyacigiller (1984) have noted, the findings of scholars from one field rarely appear to be taken into account when studies are framed in another.

The presence of several analytic levels at which organizations may be understood increases the difficulty of trying to frame a coherent theory. The differences between the disciplines are reflected, to some extent, in the levels at which organizations may be studied. Economists generally attempt to understand the behaviour of organizations as a whole or as components of large classes. Psychologists are normally more concerned with the individual or with small groups. Sociologists include both these levels, but focus heavily – especially in organizational sociology – on the organization itself as the unit of analysis.

The variety of subject areas in organizational behaviour is thus multiplied by the number of cultures in which such behaviours occur (or do not occur) and the levels at which they may be examined. For example, the recruitment of employees for international positions may be explored as an organizational function, as a requirement for effective group activation or as a cluster of individual character-istics. Such a study could be conducted in two or more countries and the results interpreted by scholars from several fields using different methods and different starting points. It is hardly surprising that there is no single underlying theory of comparative organizational behaviour.

There is one more aspect of theoretical diversity which probably contributes to the relative incoherence of the field of comparative organizational behaviour: the variety of the behaviours themselves. The field might be compared to an accumulation of stamps from around the world. There are numerous ways to categorize the stamps: by purpose, by colour, by condition, by the methods used to produce them. The first instinct of the collector is to seize on one of these categories, usually country of origin, and sort the stamps in this way. The idea of looking at the reasons for differences, the underlying conditions which lead this country to print large glossy stamps with butterflies and that one to print small sombre profiles of deceased politicians, is usually overlooked. Even the original function of the stamps, to pay for the transmission of mail, may be forgotten. So it is with comparative organizational work. The differences between nations and/or cultures are so fascinating, and the varieties so numerous, that the real task, the much more daunting task, of understanding the bases of these differences and how they influence behaviour, is neglected.

Conceptual difficulties

Though numerous conceptual difficulties are to be found in the study of comparative organizational behaviour – some common to all organizational literature, others specific to the international sphere – there is one conceptual hurdle which dominates. Almost all comparative studies, sooner or later, refer to culture. Writers are fond of citing Kroeber and Kluckhohn's (1952) review of the concept of culture, which delineated 164 separate meanings attributed to the term. Doubtless the total has increased since that book was published.

Researchers and writers have responded to this conceptual confusion in a number of ways. Some have simply declined to define culture at all. Others have used relatively simple definitions of culture, implicitly assuming that there is an underlying concept and that overelaboration only introduces interpretive difficulties. Still others have focused on particular aspects of culture. These authors generally argue that the concept is multi-dimensional and that any attempt to use a single overarching measure is doomed to failure. Rather than attempt a single definition, they define, or at least measure, particular constituents. The major difficulty with this approach is that the relationship with other dimensions of culture or with the overall concept is rarely specified.

The most radical approach to the conceptual difficulty of defining culture is Kraut's (1975) proposal that the term be dropped altogether from the vocabulary of the field. He argues that the meanings attached to the idea of culture are now so diverse, contradictory and entrenched that it is better simply to abandon the concept entirely. As with most solutions of this sort, the symptom is subjected to radical treatment, while the problem itself remains. Whatever the collection of values, traditions, routines, symbols, attitudes and signs is called, the complexity of the basic idea still poses problems for the comparative international researcher. At the same time, it will remain virtually impossible to conduct serious research without having culture or its conceptual equivalent to hand.

The many conceptualizations of culture are influenced by a number of factors, including culture itself. What is thought to comprise culture in France, its component elements and the way that they are integrated into the fabric of social interaction, will differ from the elements of Indonesian culture. If one attempts to measure culture in a society, one is faced with the problem of whether to use the local definition, one imported from another intellectual tradition or perhaps an amalgam which can be applied equally to many locales. The same problem can be found with virtually all organizational concepts. Leadership will vary across cultures, not only in the emphasis placed on leadership behaviours, but also in the basic idea of what leadership means. This type of problem can be thrown into high relief in the context of research projects utilizing personnel from several cultures. It is no less present, though it is perhaps less visible, when the research team is mono-cultural but the subjects are from several cultural traditions.

Methodological difficulties

Research in comparative organizational behaviour is prone to most of the methodological difficulties of its constituent fields. To these are added some specific problems caused by its cross-national nature. The most basic of these is the problem of sampling and the related issue of generalizability. Whatever country is studied cross-nationally, it must, perforce, be compared to some other(s). For a great many of the works in comparative organizational behaviour the base is implicitly or explicitly the home country of the researcher(s). The message is: 'Look how they do this differently over there.'

Besides the ethnocentricity of such an approach (it is 'they' who are different, not the two cultures which are mutually different), it leaves quite open the question of how either of the countries would compare to some third nation. If Spanish managers exhibit different behaviours from those of their Korean counterparts, what, if anything, does this say about the way the Spanish may differ from the Swedes, or the Koreans from the Peruvians? Many researchers assume either that such comparisons are simple extensions – that is, Spanish managers would look the same no matter whom they were compared with – or that only such simple comparisons are valid. Such extensions may have some validity, of course, but the degree of generalizability is often not considered in the design of the research.

Another difficulty in generalizing such comparisons, especially when culture is a main explanatory variable, lies in defining the boundaries of a culture. Although some work has been done which specifically recognizes the problematic relationship between national boundaries and cultural homogeneity (e.g. Tayeb 1988), most authors in the field blithely proceed as if a national entity were necessarily a cultural entity. For nations such as Canada, Switzerland, Belgium and India, this is a patently false assumption. Generalizations about cultural comparisons are unlikely to stand up if they are not even true of the original country.

Adler and Graham (1989) point out another difficulty in choosing a sample which allows useful generalization. In many studies comparing organizational behaviour, the interactions observed are between residents of a single country. These are then compared with the domestic activities of another country. If the activities are different, the conclusion is drawn that one or both sides must alter their behaviour in order for the two to work together or for one to work successfully in the other's milieu. However, Adler and Graham show, and cite other studies which show, that the way individuals behave in their own countries is often quite different from the way they behave in foreign settings. Even in their own country, their interactions with foreigners may differ markedly from their encounters with those from their own culture. To the extent that the purpose of a study is purely comparative – to understand how managers in other cultures behave differently – such generalization may be justified. When such comparisons are used as the basis for advice about interactions between cultures they may well be flawed.

Problems of generalizability are also linked to problems with the level of analysis. If one wishes to explain the behaviour of individuals in organizations and to attribute this to differences in national culture, the influence of the particular organization and the industry in which it is located should be eliminated. In addition, other organization-level factors, such as size, technology and dependence, should also be held constant. In practice, this is virtually impossible. Sampling from populations of organizations is rarely done. More commonly, researchers choose organizations which are convenient or with which they have previous connections.

There are some good, practical reasons for this tendency. Research resources, time, money and trained personnel are generally in short supply. Funding agencies in many countries are loathe to fund foreign travel for research. There may also be difficulties in sampling from a restricted universe. Some less industrialized countries may have only a few business firms of any size or sophistication, and even fewer which are locally owned and operated. Comparisons between such countries and those with larger and more developed economies, a type of research often undertaken with the aim of facilitating development, simply cannot proceed on the basis of equivalent samples. The same may be said, to a lesser degree, of comparisons between large and small industrialized countries.

There are two solutions to this problem. The first is to use matched samples. This eliminates some, though not all, of the difficulties in comparison (Hickson *et al.* 1974), but it introduces methodological considerations (Campbell and Stanley 1966) which may undermine generalizability in other ways. The most common reasons for not using matched samples are the difficulty of finding matching samples which are large enough for statistical reliability, the expense of additional travel and the difficulty of gaining entry to specific organizations.

The second option is to sample, not organizations, but individuals. A sample of participants selected randomly, without regard to organizational affiliation, may more accurately reflect the effect of national culture, since presumably all organizations of any size or located in any sector would have an equal chance of being represented. Moreover, the existence or non-existence of certain types of organizations can be seen as reflections of some of the basic values held by the inhabitants of the country, although in certain political climates and from a number of ideological perspectives this is a questionable assumption. In any case, sampling from the population of a country at large undoubtedly gives more accurate results than choosing a few organizations and claiming that their participants accurately represent the whole nation. The fact that the second approach is much more common than the first reflects the difficulties in national sampling, the added expense and, we suspect, the feeling that getting to grips with the organization itself is an essential part of the cross-cultural research process.

True comparative work often requires that the researcher(s) work in more than one language. Techniques for ensuring that instruments are equivalent, through translation and back translation, are well known but expensive, and often difficult and time-consuming. Language difficulties are less tractable when face-to-face interviews are the main means of collecting data. Not only are there difficulties in mutual understanding, but the very frame of reference imposed by the interview situation must differ from culture to culture. The context of language has its effect on both conceptualization and articulation.

We do not wish to go as far as some commentators who decry the predominance of North American (or Western) concepts and instruments (Boyacigiller and Adler 1991). The concern should not be for the origin of the methodology but for its appropriateness and utility. To assume that the methods developed in one's home country are universally applicable reflects an unacceptable and damaging level of ethnocentrism. To assume that such tools cannot be applicable in another culture seems a type of reverse ethnocentrism which is equally obtuse. The point is to understand which behaviours, values, structures, etc. are important and how they may best be measured.

A final methodological difficulty arises from the lack of a clear theoretical framework. Most comparative work, by its nature, tends to seek to identify the differences between national cultures. Hypotheses, where they exist, tend to specify that nation X should differ from nation Y in the following ways. Without a guiding theoretical framework there is a tendency to identify and explain differences while ignoring similarities. This in itself reduces the probability of establishing a theory of comparative organizational behaviour. There is a highly contradictory outcome in this. Most theories are based on regularities; that is, the relationships between variables can be seen to operate in certain predictable ways. However, the stimulus for much comparative work is the existence of a wide variety of behaviours which are caused, apparently, by widely varying factors. The rewards in the field of comparative organizational behaviour, both intellectual and material, stem mainly from the identification of specific differences and not from their inclusion in a larger theory.

THE WAY FORWARD

The considerable barriers to developing a comprehensive, or even comprehensible, theory of comparative organizational behaviour are summarized in Table 1.2. Recent proposals for advancing international and comparative research (e.g. Redding 1994; Earley and Singh 1995) have focused as much on the methods of research to be used as on the direction in which the development of theory should proceed. While the emphasis on method is understandable given the difficulties outlined above, it does seem more sensible to work toward a sound theoretical basis before considering which methods are most appropriate for testing and elaborating such a theory.

Table 1.2 Barriers to comparative research

Source of barriers	*Key problems*
Theoretical difficulties	Lack of a coherent theoretical base
	Variety of behaviours
	Diversity of approaches
	Multiple levels of analysis
	Multiple cultures
Conceptual difficulties	Multiple, conflicting definitions of culture
	Multidimensional nature of culture
	Conceptual equivalence across cultures
Methodological differences	Sampling
	Generalization
	Inference from domestic to cross-cultural settings
	Levels of analysis
	Language problems
	Focus on difference

Our agenda for the rest of the book lies in developing a cognitive approach to comparative organizational behaviour. We will begin, in Chapter 2, by examining the three traditional approaches to comparative organizational behaviour. The studies compiled under these approaches provide substantial insight into the values and processes of managers in an international context. In later chapters we will examine macro and micro issues of comparative organizational behaviour, using these considerations to develop some of the concepts for a cognitive view of comparative organizational behaviour. Our ultimate aim is not the construction of a cognitive theory; that objective is far too ambitious at this point in our project. We wish to initiate a discussion of the concepts and relationships implied by this approach, and to show how these illuminate some of the important issues facing managers in the contemporary international context.

SELECTED READINGS

Adler, N. J. (1984) 'Understanding the ways of understanding: cross-cultural management methodology reviewed', *Advances in International Comparative Management* 1: 31–67.

Adler, N. J. and Graham, J. L. (1989) 'Cross-cultural interaction: the international comparison fallacy?', *Journal of International Business Studies* 20: 515–37.

Boyacigiller, N. A. and Adler, N. J. (1991) 'The parochial dinosaur: organizational science in a global context', *Academy of Management Review* 16: 262–90.

Ghoshal, S. (1987) 'Global strategy: an organizing framework', *Strategic Management Journal* 8: 425–40.

Hofstede, G. (1985) 'The interaction between national and organizational value systems', *Journal of Management Studies* 22: 347–57.

Redding, S. G. (1994) 'Comparative management theory: jungle, zoo or fossil bed?', *Organization Studies* 15: 323–59.

Roberts, K. H. and Boyacigiller, N. A. (1984) 'Cross-national research: the grasp of the blind men', *Research in Organizational Behavior*, 6: 423–75.

Tayeb, M. (1988) *'Organizations and National Culture: A Comparative Analysis*, London: Sage.

2 Traditional approaches to comparative research

DIFFERENCES AND UNIVERSALS

The body of research on comparative organizational behaviour is so large and varied that it is virtually impossible to analyse it as a whole. In trying to separate the material into comprehensible segments critics have proposed schemes to characterize the several approaches to the field. Adler (1984), for example, categorized cross-cultural studies according to their orientation to culture, with research ranging from parochial, through polycentric to synergistic. These approaches varied in the number of cultures studied, the way in which similarities and differences were handled, and the research methodology employed. More recently, Redding (1994) classified comparative studies using two dimensions. One dimension distributes studies along an interpretive–descriptive continuum. The other runs from ideographic to nomothetic, or from micro-analysis to grand theory.

We wish to propose another categorization of comparative organizational behaviour research, one which focuses on the relationship between the work and underlying theory. In the continuing criticism of the comparative literature (Roberts 1970; Boyacigiller and Adler 1991; Redding 1994) one of the persistent themes has been the absence of a grounding theory for comparative behaviour. If the studies in the area are viewed through their relationship with theory, three approaches can be identified. The first of these traditional approaches, which we call the naive comparative, regards culture as the basic explanatory variable. Culture is seen as the motivating factor for any differences that may be observed, though the mechanism linking culture and behaviour is seldom described, much less analysed. Thus the approach is naive in the sense of being untutored or uniformed (by theory), rather than silly or foolish. Some of the studies that fall into this category are quite sophisticated, in terms of both the methodology employed and the depth of understanding generated.

The second approach rests on a secure theoretical base, that of contingency theory (Lawrence and Lorsch 1967; Thompson 1967; Pugh *et al.* 1969a, 1969b; Blau and Schoenherr 1971), which allows for comparisons of diverse types of organizations in a number of structural dimensions. The move from comparing organizations in a single society to comparing across societies was a natural one given the underlying theoretical concepts. Supporters of the culture-free approach argue that the basic tasks for any organization, especially industrial organizations, are essentially the same worldwide. Given similar circumstances the structure of the organization – the basic patterns of control, coordination and communication – can be expected to be very much the same wherever it is located (Hickson *et al.* 1974). For the culture-free school, structural similarities and the relationships among structural variables are the key issues for investigation.

While the culture-free approach seeks underlying regularities across national boundaries, the culture-bound approach emphasizes differences among cultures. However, whereas the culture-free approach is based on a single set of theories and a limited number of concepts, the culture-bound approach draws on a number of theoretical bases, especially in the fields of psychology and sociology. As with the naive comparative approach, culture is a key explanatory variable. In practice it is generally the most important, though – at least theoretically – it is one among many possible factors that may influence behaviour. Table 2.1 summarizes some of the key differences among the three approaches.

While the three traditional approaches are quite distinct conceptually, they can be somewhat difficult to differentiate in practice. The naive comparative approach is distinguished by two main characteristics: the lack of a clearly articulated theory linking culture and organizational behaviour; and the consequent emphasis on description. When it is compared to the culture-free approach the differences are usually easily discernible. The culture-free school poses one basic theoretical question: the relative similarity of organizational structures across cultural and national boundaries,

Table 2.1 Three traditional approaches to cross-cultural research

	Naive comparative	Culture-free	Culture-bound
Key research issues	How managerial functions differ	Structural similarities	Value differences; behavioural differences
View of culture	The basic explanatory variable	Explains residual variance	One key explanatory variable
Dynamics	Differentiation	Convergence	Differentiation; transference
Theoretical base	None	Contingency theory	Selected theories mainly from sociology and psychology
Major criticisms	Atheoretical; non-cumulative	Basic theory tautological; leaves too much unexplained	Weak theoretical links; lack of links between values and behaviours
Examples	Hampden-Turner and Trompenaars 1993	Hickson *et al.* 1979	Hofstede 1980a, 1991

which is based on a coherent theoretical tradition. While there may be some ambiguity in categorizing a study which makes a nod toward contingency theory before moving on to the description of cultural effects, the basic conceptual difference is clear enough.

Distinguishing between the naive comparative and culture-bound approaches is more problematic. Both approaches focus on differences in organizational behaviour to be found between cultures and countries. While the culture-bound approach is theory-driven, there is no single school or set of theories which dominates. At base the key distinction between the two approaches lies in explanation. The naive comparative approach attributes differences in behaviour or attitudes – to the extent that such differences are explained at all – to concepts such as culture, national character or social factors. Causal links are not specified. The culture-free approach supplies, sometimes quite sketchily, not only a cause for the observed differences but also some link between cause and effect.

An illustrative comparison can be drawn between the naive comparative work of Hampden-Turner and Trompenaars (1993) and Hofstede's culture-bound research (1980a, 1991). The studies are both derived from large data bases. Employees (managers for Hampden-Turner and Trompenaars, employees from all levels for Hofstede) were asked their opinions on a number of issues thought to reflect certain basic social values. Hampden-Turner and Trompenaars link their findings on individual questions to business practices and illustrate their insights with anecdotes, literary references and cases. Hofstede reduces a large number of items to overarching dimensions, which he then links to various psychological constructs. Both books provide important insights into various cultures, but for Hampden-Turner and Trompenaars the links between values and behaviour are country-specific. The Dutch believe in group planning because of their historic efforts to protect themselves from the sea. For Hofstede, the link between authoritarianism and social distance holds for all cultures. To be sure, the boundary between the two approaches is not precise, but the conceptual difference is crucial to understanding the field.

The internationalist view of a diverse world

In addition to the three traditional approaches to comparative organizational behaviour a new approach to understanding international management has emerged over the past decade. It is not, strictly speaking, comparative, although its agenda is shaped by the diversity that emerges from cultural variation. Whereas the three comparative approaches are concerned with the occurrence of behavioural differences among societies, the internationalist approach takes these as background and seeks ways to manage effectively international functions which must operate across cultural barriers. In some ways this is a return to a centrist view of the international corporation since the desired result is better training for those managers who must operate in a global setting, usually those based at headquarters.

This emerging approach differs from older centrist approaches in time horizon and cultural specificity. In older, centrist views the manager was seen as someone who would be posted, normally as a senior manager, to a subsidiary for several years. He or she needed training in the ways of the local culture, especially in the types of interactions that would occur with local staff. Preliminary training and advice on adaptation were focused on one particular country or, at most, a region. The internationalist approach, reflecting the management strategies employed by global firms, has a much shorter time horizon. International managers, when electronic communication will not suffice, travel from country to country, seldom staying more than a few months in any one place. There is no time and little perceived need for detailed briefings or prolonged accommodation to a particular culture. What the manager needs, and what internationalist research should identify, are traits and skills which allow quick adaptation to a series of new environments. There is an emphasis on policies and systems that allow control of functions from headquarters with occasional personal intervention. Given this centrist point of view it is not surprising that much of the research in this tradition is conducted at headquarters or at least in the home country. The views of managers who pull the firm's international levers are solicited on which qualities make a good transnational manager or what factors provide effective global policies. Opinions are seldom sought from those being managed outside the home country.

The academic foundations of the internationalist approach also differ from those of the more traditional views. As indicated in Table 2.2, the internationalists rarely stray outside the boundaries of management for their theoretical and methodological tools. Not surprisingly, areas closely identified with management theories, such as leadership and human resource management, have received the most attention. The demands of the global corporation have meant that leaders, especially those at the very top of the organization, must appeal to a wide range of employees, clients and investors. With the advent of satellite communication and mass-produced videos these leaders can and do appear simultaneously to audiences around the world. Knowing what is universally leader-like looms as a serious problem for such managers. Similarly, emphasis on the effective utilization of human resources on a global scale means that fragmented personnel policies tailored to specific countries are both ineffective and inefficient. If managers and technical personnel are to be moved about the world as needed, then a system that will be perceived as equitable – both internally and

Table 2.2 Comparative and internationalist approaches

	Comparative approach	Internationalist approach
Key issue	Value and behavioural differences across cultures	The traits, skills and strategies needed for international management
Role of culture	Basic explanatory variable	Source of environmental diversity
Source of change	Cultural divergence or convergence	International growth of organization
Conceptual roots	Anthropology, sociology, psychology	Management
Managerial time horizon	Moderate to long	Short
Managerial application	To prepare managers for assignments abroad	To set up and operate international management functions
Examples	Hofstede 1991; Hickson and Pugh 1995	Kets de Vries and Mead 1992; S. Taylor *et al.* 1996

externally – is required. In both cases local adaptation must give way to international uniformity, at least at the level of policy and systems.

Since the internationalist approach is not directly concerned with comparative issues it will receive little direct analysis in this book, although some studies in this vein are discussed in Chapter 5. It has been mentioned here because it has emerged as a rival to the traditional approaches as a source of managerial advice and instruction concerning the problems of international management. It also reflects the evolution, in light of globalization, of two themes from earlier approaches; that is, the centrist perspective of the naive comparative view and the universalist tendencies of the culture-free school. As we turn our attention to a more detailed analysis of the three traditional approaches, the challenge of the internationalists and the contrasting assumptions they invoke should be seen as providing an implicit criticism of the work produced by comparative researchers.

THE NAIVE COMPARATIVE APPROACH: COMPARED TO WHAT?

Detailed discussion of even a small portion of the naive comparative *oeuvre* is problematic because of the diversity of topics covered, its geographic scope and the highly variable quality of the work. There are, however, two features of the approach which not only illustrate its strengths and weaknesses, but also provide a rough map of its implications for comparative organizational behaviour. The first of these is the basic comparison inherent in the approach. The countries or cultures involved in the comparison may be chosen for a number of reasons. Several countries have, at different times and for different reasons, served as a central focus for comparative work. Some of these have simply represented the home country of a researcher who, for some reason or another, finds himself or herself abroad – this has been called 'vacation empiricism' (Steers *et al.* 1992). Other countries have been of interest because they help position the subject country or focus on a particular problem, for example innovation, international competitiveness or labour relations. Still others, such as Japan, Saudi Arabia and, more recently, Middle European and East Asian countries, have received concerted attention through their changing economic or strategic importance.

In recent years there has been a further development within which specific managerial functions or organizational properties have been targeted in naive comparative studies. This appears to be an effort to overcome the difficulty of generating specific practical recommendations from more general comparisons. By focusing on particular management problems such as leadership, organizational development or decision-making, researchers can tighten the scope of the analysis and target recommendations more narrowly. While this provides useful information in a binational setting, it also exacerbates one of the serious limitations of the naive comparative approach, a lack of generalizability.

Country characteristics and comparisons

For naive comparisons which are purposeful – that is, which represent something beyond an opportunistic study – at least one of the countries must represent a baseline. Comparisons seldom include regional or cross-national cultural units, although some are included within the culture-bound approach (e.g. Chanlat and Bedard 1991). The point of comparison often arises from a specific characterization of the country. A number of these have proven popular in different eras. For example, the long tradition of Anglo–US comparisons (Jamieson 1980) reflects a general characterization of the United Kingdom as the seat of the Industrial Revolution and hence traditional in both its management practices and its work arrangements. The United States, for a good deal of the post-war era, was characterized as aggressive, expansionary, innovative and, above all, successful. Servain-Schreiber's (1968) recommendation of the American multinational model to European businesses was an early and highly influential example of this point of view.

Sweden has often been used as a point of comparison for naive research because of its reputation for innovative industrial relations approaches embedded in a society with a strong emphasis on economic equality. Yugoslavia was, for a substantial period before its disintegration, used as an example of a culture in which workers' control played a strong role in organizational operations (e.g. Drenth *et al.* 1979). In this it was often used as a proxy for other Eastern and Central European centrally planned economies, which were, until recently, less available for direct observation and research. India has frequently been used in the literature as an example of a developing country. This stems partly from the domestic tradition of organizational research in India and the work available from scholars visiting there.

The current focus is, of course, on Japan and the Pacific Rim countries (see Dunphy 1986 for an early summary of the literature). Obvious international success, a distinct social basis for organization and impressive rates of innovation have all led to an intense interest, which was initially magnified by a very low level of knowledge about Japanese management practice.

For the most part the salient features of these characterizations are assumed by researchers. There is very seldom any evidence in a study that, for example, the particular US firm being studied is actually innovative or that a Swedish firm is kind to its workers. Thus, what is to be explained in these studies is often assumed to be true, rather than tested. This means that many of the naive comparative studies provide information about the differences between the organizations or individuals included but little about the cultures in which they are embedded. The accumulation of results and subsequent generalization from this approach become problematic. Recent events, including the decline of US economic hegemony and the violent break-up of Yugoslavia, raise questions as to how culturally grounded the original characterizations really were.

The new world and the old

A popular contrast in the comparative literature has been the United Kingdom and the United States. This has been facilitated by three factors: a common language, the role of the two countries in the international economy and their position as the site of much of the early work on organizational behaviour. The fact that both nations have a long tradition of foreign investment also meant that problems of coordinating across multiple cultures posed a set of immediate problems for managers in both countries.

An early exemplar of the naive comparative approach can be found in Dubin's 'Management in Britain: impressions of a visiting professor' (1970). In this paper Dubin addresses the question of why the 'tremendous demonstrated potential for industrial development and technical innovation in the U.K. today' (Dublin 1970: 183) has not been fully realized. This focus is typical in that the author believes that UK management need only be adjusted to become more productive. Second, the appropriate comparison, the United States, is felt to be so obvious that little justification is needed; the basis of the comparison is not mentioned in the title even though the article was published in a British journal. The key ingredient in US superiority, Dubin believes, is to be found in its commitment to innovation.

Dubin proposes that key differences are located in three general areas: the attitudes and values of executives, the social structure of British industry and British management style. These three areas are then expanded into eight features, on which the two countries are compared. The eight features are perfectibility, professionalization, class position, age-grading, managerial mobility, resource allocation, personal trust and 'personalistic' relations. Comparing businesses in the two countries using these eight categories, Dubin observes that their industrial cultures are quite different.

This article is typical of both the naive approach and the general approach to US–UK comparisons. Most readers could predict how each country would perform on the eight features based on their general characterizations. There is no data in Dubin's article to support his assertions; they are, as the title indicates, simply impressions. Nor is there any empirical link between these eight features and innovative behaviour. It is assumed that having younger managers in positions of power will lead to more innovative behaviour, but there is no evidence to support that assumption generally, nor to indicate that it holds in this particular instance.

What is left is little more than a caricature. It is, to be sure, the type of caricature that inhabits the cognitive maps of most managers and many academics. In that sense it may reflect the experience of managers who work abroad. However, the exercise provides no specific findings, no data and carries no particular theoretical interest.

More recently the US has often been compared with Japan. In contrast to Dubin's characterization of the US as an innovative, dynamic industrial power, it is now portrayed as struggling and somewhat backward, with Japanese management techniques providing many of the possible answers to its problems. 'Spurred on by Japanese competition, American managers have looked seriously at culture for answers to sluggish productivity growth, poor quality, and fading competitive capability' (Peterson *et al.* 1994: 77). Contrasted with the highly positive views portrayed by Servain-Schreiber (1968) and Dubin, this presents quite a different picture. Three issues are raised by this change in the characterization of US business. First, what is the relationship between the economic context of comparisons and underlying cultural values? The clear implication of Dubin's article is that British managers (and industry) should strive to be more like their American counterparts. For Peterson and her colleagues, as well as a number of authors they cite, the conclusion is just the opposite. This does not in itself imply that the underlying values of US society have changed (see Hampden-Turner and Trompenaars 1993), but it certainly implies that the way values are viewed by researchers, and perhaps by managers themselves, has changed.

The second issue involves the relationship between values and success. Since cultures vary in the emphasis put on business success, the expression of values may also vary depending on the degree to which they are perceived as being linked to success. The re-evaluation of individualist versus collectivist approaches to work which is now occurring in North America may indicate a shift in the type of managerial behaviours valued. Whether this indicates an underlying shift in values remains to be seen, but the direct link between collectivist practices in organizations and collectivist values in, for example, Japanese culture is one that many naive comparative researchers have been quite willing to make on the basis of little or no specific evidence.

Finally, the accepted view of a particular country or society may also depend on the standpoint from which it is examined. There are two aspects to this. First, the type of contrasts that may emerge will differ. The naive approach is typically much more concerned with observed differences in managerial behaviour than with similarities. The types of differences that would emerge in a comparison of Danish and Nigerian managers would likely diverge from those identified in a contrast of Canadian and Brazilian managers. Even for comparisons which focus on a single country the stance of the observer may have important effects on the outcome of the research. Shifting the vantage point for viewing the United States from the United Kingdom in the 1970s to Japan in the 1990s will certainly alter the features that dominate the cultural landscape.

These difficulties can be illustrated by comparing two studies which involved US managers as the empirical baseline. In an examination of Saudi Arabian and US management values, Al-Aiban and Pearce begin from the following characterization:

> [Saudi Arabia] provides a clear contrast to American society, which is dominated by ideals that are based on what Weber called bureaucratic authority: the universal application of rules or law, positions according to merit (determined by objective means, if possible), promotion based on individual performance, and clear rules governing the limitations of authority.
>
> (Al-Aiban and Pearce 1993: 38)

Their hypotheses suggest that Saudi managers will be more traditional and less bureaucratic than their American counterparts. Al-Aiban and Pearce used five categories of attitudes to distinguish between the two cultures: rule-boundedness, non-merit evaluation criteria, nepotism, goal clarity and job as personal property. They found differences on the first three of these.

A study which included managers from Japan, Taiwan, Mexico and the United States characterized US managers in the following way: 'Hand in hand with individualism, goal attainment and a future orientation is the view that time is limited and therefore valuable'

(Kelley *et al*. 1987: 24). Differences among the four cultures were sought on twelve dimensions, among which were self-motivation, long-term employment, cooperation and respect for formal authority. Significant differences were found between the Japanese and Americans, while contrasts between the Americans and the Taiwanese, and Americans and Mexicans were less distinguishable.

These two studies demonstrate some of the difficulties that arise from trying to draw even the most immediate and practical conclusions from naive comparisons. The characterizations of the United States which underlie the contrasts are not necessarily contradictory, but they emphasize different aspects of US culture and, in some cases, different levels of analysis. The bureaucratic, rule-based values on which Al-Aiban and Pearce base their comparison are located at the societal and organizational levels. In the Weberian version that they utilize, these values provide for the articulation between the two levels. For Kelley and his colleagues, the important differences may be found at the level of individual values such as respect for authority and self-motivation, or in organizational practices such as long-term employment, centralized decision-making and written procedures. Because the two studies focus on different levels their authors are led to emphasize different aspects of culture; this, in turn, leads to hypotheses which are not additive or even comparable. On the one hand, this diversity of approach is useful since it provides a more complete picture of the possible effects of culture on the organization and its members. On the other hand, it makes the integration of results more akin to assembling a three-dimensional puzzle than to accumulating repeated tests of similar hypotheses.

The orientation of the two studies and the results obtained may also differ because they are aimed at different parts of the cultural equation. Al-Aiban and Pearce are concerned with the interaction of public- and private-sector differences and cultural variation. Kelley *et al*. focus more on the transference and persistence of culture between societies. Two other studies which are closer in purpose – and, by coincidence, were conducted using the same three countries – provide another useful contrast of naive comparative techniques. Kim *et al*. (1990) compared attitudes on reward allocations using students from the United States, Japan and Korea. Dubinksy *et al*. (1991) used managers from the same three countries to examine the ethical perceptions of salespeople.

The Dubinsky *et al.* study posed to the sample of managers three questions concerning twelve ethical situations. The subjects were supposed to consider whether or not the situations involved an ethical dilemma, and to report whether the subject's firm had a policy on the topic and whether they thought it should have such a policy. Significant country effects were found among the countries on all three questions, although the particular contrasts between pairs of countries were significant for different sets of situations. In the US–Japan comparisons the US salespeople found the situations to pose fewer ethical issues but claimed more often that their firms had policies covering situations and that the policies were required. These differences were attributed to the paternal nature of the Japanese corporation, with its interwoven web of group commitments, against the more formal framework governing the behaviour of American salespeople.

The research of Kim and his colleagues focused on the distribution of awards for behaviours. The study was a relatively straightforward survey of attitudes given varying scenarios. Interestingly, the study found a common commitment to equity across all three cultures. However, the Japanese and American subjects were closer to each other than to the Koreans. The lack of a significant difference between the Japanese and Americans is explained in terms of Hofstede's (1980a) individualism and masculinity dimensions rather than any specific cultural referents.

The contrast in findings between these two studies can be attributed to a number of circumstances. While both used similar methodologies, the Kim *et al.* study used university students and Dubinsky *et al.* surveyed salespeople. Moreover, some of the questions for the salespeople related to actual practice rather than projected behaviours. Nonetheless, it is interesting that on related behaviours which ought to be linked to deeper cultural values the two studies arrive at nearly opposite conclusions regarding the similarity of the three cultures involved. This points to two major difficulties with the naive comparative approach. First, there is the unexamined assumption that cultural differences exist. Neither of these studies anchors its theoretical expectations in specific cultural phenomena. Second, there is no underlying theoretical framework within which these results can be consolidated. Thus the varied studies of US management practices summarized in Table 2.3 (which are, of course, only a small portion of those available) exhibit

Table 2.3 Representative naive comparative studies

Issue	Study	Cultures examined	Findings
The effects of values on practices	Al-Aiban and Pearce 1993	Saudi Arabia, the United States	Some differences reported
The effect of culture on values	Kelley *et al.* 1987	Japan, Mexico, Taiwan, the United States	Differences between Japan and the United States
Attitudes toward rewards	Kim *et al.* 1990	Japan, Korea, the United States	Koreans differed from Japan and the United States
Attitudes toward ethics	Dubinsky *et al.* 1991	Japan, Korea, the United States	Differences among all three countries

a contradictory view of the American managerial culture even when the countries with which it is being compared are held constant.

Evaluation

What we have called the naive comparative approach to cross-national research has been severely criticized, implicitly and explicitly, by many commentators (e.g. Barrett and Bass 1976; Boyacigiller and Adler 1991; Redding 1994). The most persistent criticism is the absence of any theoretical basis for the comparisons which lie at the centre of the naive comparative effort. Lacking a clear conceptual framework, these studies lead to results that are non-cumulative and contribute little to the development of the field. In the same vein, these studies are criticized for being merely descriptive. Detailed discussions of specific differences in organizational or behavioural phenomena, while useful, require careful analysis if they are to realize their full theoretical and prescriptive potential. Moreover, these studies have been criticized for highlighting differences without weighing up contrasts and similarities to assess the distance between cultures and nations.

All of these criticisms are warranted. However, the implication that is often drawn from them – that these studies can make no contribution to the development of a theory of comparative organizational behaviour – is not. The studies which fall into this category vary widely. It appears that they still comprise a substantial portion of published work in the field. They range from comparisons which are little more than received wisdom (which often contain persistent misconceptions) to methodologically sophisticated and subtly argued studies. The best of these studies provide two important inputs in the search for a coherent approach to comparative organizational behaviour.

The first is great breadth of coverage. There are few countries which have escaped the naive comparative net. Some, such as Japan, the United States and the United Kingdom, have been compared to numerous other countries and cultures. A comprehensive theory of comparative organizational behaviour requires that behaviours from the widest variety of national and cultural settings be included. The vast body of data emanating from naive comparisons presents a good indication of the range of behaviours that must be accommodated. If the development of a paradigm – or, more modestly, comprehensive middle range theories (Redding 1994) – is the goal, then it is more likely to emerge from a consideration of these numerous studies than from an exercise which begins *de novo*.

Second, the body of naive comparisons often provides methodological triangulation for descriptions of organizational behaviour. Work involving case studies, surveys or attitudinal data is to be found for many countries. Comparisons of a particular country with several others, in either binational or multiple comparisons, provide contrasting views. Multiple levels of analysis, especially at the individual and organizational levels, help provide a comparative picture of great richness. The contrasting approaches of separate researchers and teams from different countries give a rounded picture of organizational behaviour. Any finding which consistently emerges from this multiplicity of methods and sources has a strong claim to validity. Finally, it must be said that the naive comparative approach does not, as yet, provide any indication of how important cultural differences are in explaining behaviour or how such differences lead to action. The approach remains resolutely surface-oriented.

CULTURE-FREE: AN OIL REFINERY IS AN OIL REFINERY IS AN OIL REFINERY

The second of the traditional approaches we wish to examine, the culture-free approach, differs sharply from the naive comparative.

Whereas the naive comparative begins from an appreciation of difference, the culture-free focuses on similarities. The naive comparative approach eschews theory, while the culture-free approach has its roots in a well-documented theoretical framework, contingency theory, which initially had little connection with comparative issues. Instead of focusing on the surface contrasts that the naive comparative authors believe reflect deeper differences, the culture-free theorists believe that there is an underlying similarity between organizations facing the same tasks in the same environment anywhere in the world. From the culture-free view an oil refinery in Indonesia will resemble one in Canada or in Venezuela in most important aspects.

The transfer of technology, the growth and management of multinational corporations (MNCs), the design of global and regional products, and international strategy formation all seem to be predicated on the notion that the similarities in organizational functioning in cultures across the world outweigh any differences. This approach to cross-cultural management assumes that any difficulties encountered can be regarded as minor and local and can be ignored or accommodated in some way. Thus the impact of national values and other societal effects are insignificant; what is important is the task, the technologies used to accomplish it and the environments that organizations face.

To explore the idea that organizations are essentially culture-free we will briefly outline its origins in the convergence thesis and discuss the notion of a universalist theory of organizational structure which gave rise to it. The idea of a universalist theory is implicit in what was for a time the most prominent theoretical framework in organization analysis, contingency theory. We will look at how this framework, together with a set of well-operationalized measures and multivariate statistical techniques, has shaped this strand of comparative management research. We then discuss one of the key exemplars of this strand of thinking, the Aston Studies, particularly the development and testing of the 'bold hypothesis' of convergence of organizational forms.

The importance of the culture-free approach is evaluated in several ways. We first examine the evidence for a stable pattern of relationships of structural variables across nations. We then explore the meaning of stability, examine measurement problems and ask if contingency theory itself may be flawed. Finally, we discuss the relationship, or lack of it, between organizational structure and individual behaviour.

The origins of the 'bold hypothesis'

The basic hypothesis of the culture-free approach has its roots in the convergence debate inaugurated by Clark Kerr and his colleagues at Harvard University in the 1960s (Kerr *et al.* 1960; see also Pugh and Hickson 1996). They argued that industrialization is a worldwide phenomenon based on science and technology. Science is seen as supranational, independent of the form of government or the culture of a people. Technology diffuses so that the world is apparently divided into those countries which are industrialized and those which are in the process of becoming so. In Kerr's view, the movement toward industrialization is an inevitable transition. The worldwide diffusion of science and technology creates a 'logic of industrialism' since it sets up a range of tasks and problems which must be addressed. Competitive pressures towards efficient production ensure that the most effective ways of tackling these common tasks will eventually come to be adopted worldwide. As competitive industrialization continues, organizations tackling the same tasks will become more and more alike, regardless of the culture in which they are embedded.

Perhaps the most significant of these developmental forces, at least for comparative analysis, is the emergence of organizations on a scale large enough to combine effectively the various factors of production. The success of organization-building depends on the development of managerial capability, which leads to increasing specialization of the functions through which managers control the production process. One way in which managers exert effective control is by establishing consistent patterns of rules and procedures to effect control, coordination and communication, i.e. by developing an organizational structure. As organizations grow in size they tend to become structured in standard ways.

The bold hypothesis of structural convergence echoes the 'one best way of organizing' theme found in the classical management school (e.g. F. W. Taylor 1947; Fayol 1949). The classical theorists advocated a simple set of principles (coupled, in Taylor's case, with a detailed methodology) thought to be applicable to any task. Yet the experience of both managers and researchers led to questions of how universal such theories could be. Hickson *et al.* pose the question as follows: 'How far is organization theory an American edifice fabricated on a foundation of Western European Weberian thought? How far is it relevant to Asia, Africa or wherever?' (Hickson *et al.* 1979: 25). If theories of organizational structure are not universal, should the focus be on culturally specific theories of organization? However daunting this prospect may be (J. Lincoln *et al.* 1986), social scientists continue to build and test theories which are universal in the sense that they are believed to apply across cultures and nations.

Contingency theory

The framework of contingency theory began as a challenge to the 'one best way' or early universalist view. Joan Woodward and her colleagues found that organizations in their British sample exhibited a variety of structural configurations, which they attributed to the technologies the organizations employed (Woodward 1965). These results were easily interpreted as supporting the convergence hypothesis since changes in technology are a normal result of industrialization.

The implications of the work on strategy and structure that was emerging at about the same time were more problematic for a universalist approach. This group of studies, following Chandler's (1962) thesis, links growth strategies to organization structure. They consistently found that 'those companies that diversified into related and unrelated businesses overwhelmingly chose multi-divisional structures' (Galbraith and Nathanson 1979: 253). They report that when the same type of analysis was undertaken for firms in the UK (Channon 1973) and continental Europe (Dyas and Thanheiser 1976) it was found that an increase in diversification was accompanied by an increase in the use of the multi-divisional structure compared to functional and holding-company arrangements. Scott summed up this stream of research when he argued that 'overall, both in strategy and structure, the European companies appear headed the same way as their US competitors' (B. R. Scott 1973: 141). This indicated that there was some convergence across countries but that alternative strategic choices might lead to deviations in structure.

Gradually the view that organizational structure was contingent on a number of factors, including technology and strategy, became the dominant strand in macro organizational theory, as near to a paradigm as the field has ever achieved. The research agenda consisted of identifying important features of organizational structure, such as coordinating mechanisms (Lawrence and Lorsch 1967), and relating them to each other as well as to other potential contingent factors, such as environmental richness (Child 1972). Contingency theory became entrenched as the new orthodoxy.

This basic and familiar argument suggests that, if they are to be successful, organizations must be structured in response to a series of demands or contingencies posed by the scale of operations, usually expressed as size, the technology employed and the environment within which operations take place. Thus variance in organizational structure is due primarily to the contingencies faced and not to societal or cultural location. The perceived wisdom of the convergence view is that any deviation from this pattern is explained by the fact that some organizations (in some cultures) have yet to catch up, in structural terms, with contingencies (Pugh 1989).

Research resulting from this conjunction of concepts and tools is perhaps best exemplified by the work of Derek Pugh and the Aston Group (Pugh and Hickson 1976; Pugh and Hinings 1976). The wealth of data generated by this approach led to another 'bold hypothesis' (Hickson *et al.* 1974). It was bold in the sense that it was simple but offered a starting point for comprehensive comparative research. This proposition, essentially the convergence thesis restated in structural terms, was examined in a large number of studies from numerous locales. One of these (Inkson *et al.* 1981) contrasted samples of US and UK managers. Unlike Dubin, they found that 'these similarities in managerial aspirations are paralleled by close similarities in managers' perceptions of roles, and in organization structure' (*ibid.*: 36). In this they go beyond the core of the contingency approach to imply that structure also shapes the ways in which managers perceive their functions.

Other studies (summarized in Table 2.4) delivered similar results. Child and Kieser (1981), for example, found that both German and British firms exhibited the relationships hypothesized in contingency theory, although they did perceive the influence of culture on levels of decentralization and the relative strength of the associations among structural variables. A study of American and Nigerian organizations found that 'virtually all of the results reported in this paper suggest the similarities of comparable organizations functioning in quite

Table 2.4 Representative culture-free studies

Issue	Study	Cultures examined	Findings
Structural relationships	Inkson *et al.* 1981	The United Kingdom, the United States	Similar associations among structural variables
Structural relationships	Child and Kieser 1981	Germany, the United Kingdom	Similar associations among structural variables, except centralization
Distribution of authority	W. R. Scott *et al.* 1979	Nigeria, the United States	Similar allocations of authority
The effect of culture on administrative bureaucracies	Aiken and Bacharach 1979	French and Walloon areas in Belgium	No structural differences

different settings' (W. R. Scott *et al.* 1979: 179). An intriguing study by Aiken and Bacharach (1979) investigated the structure of local-government bureaucracies in the French and Walloon sectors of Belgium. They found that, while culture affected some of the administrative processes, it did not affect structural characteristics. As do most of the other studies in this theoretical stream, they acknowledge the importance of culture but find that it does not influence organizational structure.

Meta-analyses of culture-free studies

The existence of numerous studies using similar methodologies allowed for an overall assessment of the effect of culture on organizational structures. Hickson and McMillan (1981) gathered together a number of studies which had applied the Aston programme in different countries. The papers did not emerge from a coordinated research effort; some were opportunistic, some comprised a segment of other studies. Examining the data, Hickson and McMillan conclude that it is possible to explain the different pattern of scores in various countries in terms of 'the time and speed of economic development, and of the management consequences of state planning' (Hickson and McMillan 1981: 192). However, does this explanation apply in all countries?

They observe consistent positive relationships between organization size and the structural variables of degree of specialization and formalization. They also point out the repeated positive relation between the centralization of decision-making and the degree of interorganizational dependence. These, taken together, form a 'focal paradigm of relationships which, . . . could help to form a stable core to organization theory' (Hickson and McMillan 1981: 193). This notion of the stable paradigm is one that Hickson and his co-workers have promulgated in almost every summary of the Aston approach. However, in this piece Hickson and McMillan point out that the notion of culture-free structural relationships 'does not mean that context is a sort of glacial deposit from nowhere. . . . Context is chosen; and that choice may be culturally influenced' (*ibid.*: 194). This allows for cultural influence on structures, but not at the level of the individual or the organization. This fails to address the question of who is making the choices that affect societal constraints (Child 1972; Maurice 1979).

Hickson and McMillan proceed further into the debate by suggesting that one choice, for example on state intervention into industrial policy, constrains the next choice. While there is some evidence to suggest a hierarchy of decisions (Schendel and Hofer 1979; Mallory and Cray 1982), determination of size probably occurs more as a result of strategy implementation than of conscious choice. The conclusion suggested by Hickson and McMillan (1981) is that the underlying relationships or paradigm act as a set of parameters within which culturally influenced choices can occur. '[T]he Aston methods offer means to study context–structure relationships, allowing the teasing out of the clinical side of organizational processes which reveal most fully the cultural variations' (*ibid.*: 196), but only longitudinal data will reveal whether or not convergence is occurring (c.f. Maurice 1979).

Their review, Hickson and McMillan (1981) argue, demonstrates the stable pattern of relationships between variables that Hickson *et al.* had deemed so important to the study of organizations as this would 'help to clarify the part played by nationality or custom or culture' (Hickson *et al.* 1979: 30). Perhaps the pattern did not prove to be as stable as appearances first suggested.

First, in this context, what does stability actually mean? According to Child, 'high, consistent correlations across societies do not, of course, demonstrate stability in the form of context structure relationships since the regression slopes may differ' (Child 1981: 314). He goes on to suggest that such differences could indicate the 'influence of cultural preferences for particular forms of organization' (*ibid.*). In essence this is the strategic choice argument restated in Maurice's (1979) terms. As many of the inferences drawn by Hickson *et al.* (1979) and Hickson and McMillan (1981) follow this methodology, how are we to evaluate their conclusions?

Their attempt to integrate the findings of various studies is one form of what has come to be known as meta-analysis (Hunter *et al.* 1982), which is an attempt to accumulate knowledge across studies. A more statistically robust analysis of these relationships was performed by Donaldson, who used data from published studies and the Aston data bank 'to enquire into the issue of generalizability more deeply than the previous reviews. It [his paper] examines whether the inconsistencies are more apparent than real' (Donaldson 1986: 70). Donaldson was especially concerned with the possible role of sampling error in and across the various studies. He also considered whether or not any remaining variation was due to moderating variables. He proposed two possible moderators: organizational type, divided into manufacturing and service; and geo-political area. He argued that there would be differences in degree, for example in the size–centralization relationship for organizations located in the West compared with those in the East. Organization type and Westernness according to Donaldson, 'stand as proxies for two underlying theoretical moderators of the size–bureaucracy relationship: routineness of operations and managerial independence' (*ibid.*: 71). This, in itself, represents a heroic simplification of cultural tendencies in highly diverse cultures, which may indicate the level of sophistication with which cultural concepts are treated in the culture-free approach.

We can summarize the findings of this well-argued paper in Table 2.5, which shows that the size–specialization relationship holds across organizational type and across the globe. Both standardization and formalization are significantly affected by organizational type, being lower in service organizations than in manufacturing. Westernness has no moderating effect. The correlations between size and centralization scores hold across organizational type but exhibit

Table 2.5 Summary of Donaldson's (1986) findings on size and bureaucracy

Structure Variables	Moderator variables	
	Organization Type	Westernness
Specialization	Not significant	Not significant
Standardization	Significant	Not significant
Formalization	Significant	Not significant
Centralization	Not significant	Significant

differences across Westernness, although that difference is not enough to change the direction of the relationship. As Donaldson (1986) points out, the relationship between size and centralization is weak and more subject to variation than the overall size–structure relationships. There are three anomalous findings for this size–centralization relationship. The three countries were Canada, Japan and Sweden. For these three the relationship was positive. Donaldson's position seems to be that, while there may be weak moderator effects, they serve only to reduce the size of the association not to reverse its sign: 'There are valid general relationships between size and organization structure' (*ibid.*: 89), but this conclusion can at best be only tentative and 'subject to qualifications . . . they are offered only as an initial exploration of the issues' (*ibid.*: 91).

In another examination of the relationships between size and organization structure across countries, G. A. Miller also used meta-analysis in an attempt to overcome the 'tentative, equivocal and contradictory conclusions' (G. A. Miller 1987: 313) that previous studies, usually based on narrative reviews, had produced. He, too, looked for the effect of moderator variables and picked two that are similar to Donaldson's. Miller employs type of organization, although he separates this into manufacturing and other (unspecified) types. The second classification was into Anglo-Saxon countries and others, a somewhat simpler version of Donaldson's Westernness categorization. Miller concludes that the relationship between size and specialization is a substantial one, and, as with Donaldson, neither organization type nor country appears significantly to moderate this relationship. For the relationship between size and formalization, type of organization does account for some of the differences in the observed correlations, but it is not an important moderator. As with specialization, country does not exert substantial effects on this relationship. These findings essentially concur with Donaldson's analysis; however, Miller does suggest that the 'relationship between size and centralization is different' (*ibid.*: 318). Across the studies the relationship 'is not significantly different from zero' (*ibid.*). While this conclusion does not differ too sharply from that drawn by Donaldson (see above), it states it more forcefully and prompts a closer analysis of this relationship. Miller also claims that 'it would appear that there has always been some "problem" with this indicator' (*ibid.*: 319).

What is also interesting is how two additional quantitative meta-analyses have focused on the relationship between size and centralization, and not the more familiar one between dependence and centralization. For Child, the structural dimension, centralization, is the one 'most likely to reflect differences in philosophies of control, norms on authority relationships and other potentially culture-related managerial outlooks' (Child 1981: 314). Indeed he goes on to say that 'in respect of centralization of decision making the total collection of cross-national studies which have employed comparable measures do not demonstrate either a strong or consistent relationship with dependence which is "stable across societies"' (*ibid.*: 315). Indeed, there may even be instabilities within the same country. Child suggests that the presence of American- and European-owned subsidiaries in the sample may have had an impact on the relationships found. This leads to the tentative conclusion that in some way culture is a moderator here. Indeed, both Jamieson (1980) and Mallory *et al.* (1983), who studied the operation of American subsidiaries in the UK, suggest that there are distinctive differences in mode of operation between them and comparable UK companies. Blankenburg, in his review of Hickson and McMillan (1981), suggests that centralization varies more with national specifics 'than with organizational universals' (Blankenburg 1983: 388). So it appears that at least three dimensions of organization structure and the relationship with size exhibit the same pattern across societies. Yet there appears to be some remaining variation not due to sampling error or moderator effects that needs explanation.

In addition to critiques of the cross-cultural consistency of basic structural relationships, the underlying logic of the whole contingency approach has frequently been criticized. Perhaps the most informed and cogent critique of this approach was provided by Starbuck (1981). He questioned the meaning and validity of some of the key variables, the reliability of the data and the problems of aggregating the various measures into scales. He also addressed some more serious issues which impinge on notions of a universal and generalizable theory. There are other related critical issues. For example, Aldrich (1972) examined the causal logic underlying the size, technology and structure relationship. He argued, from a path analysis of the Aston data set, that size, in fact, depends on structuring of activities. Hilton (1972) went further, and found the Aston data to be consistent with three distinct causal models.

In a more general vein, other authors have gone much further in their critique of contingency approaches to organization structure (but see Donaldson 1985 for a spirited defence). For example, Salaman argues that 'conventional organization theory, by "discovering" causal relationships which reveal the inevitability of current organizational forms, becomes so embedded within, and celebratory of, these forms as to be unable to envisage alternative structures' (Salaman 1978: 520). He goes on to suggest that attention should be paid to 'the political, sectional nature of apparently neutral procedures and technology' (*ibid.*). The contingency approach does not recognize that structures, and the rules that embody them, are the product of the underlying rationality of the ruling elite and, as such, are thus culturally bound. The assumptions underpinning such rationalities are neither questioned nor explored by work done under the aegis of contingency theory. The work of both Child (1972, 1981) and Maurice (1979) already cited draws our attention to this issue by arguing that, at the very least, the culture–politics nexus is a reality of organization structure and process.

Evaluation

The popularity of the culture-free approach has declined in recent years. Since the publication of the compilation edited by Hickson and McMillan (1981) and the Lammers and Hickson compendium (1979a), which included some strong arguments for the importance of a universalistic theory of organizational structure, cross-national thinking and research have resolutely focused on difference rather than similarity, on explicit behaviour rather than deeper structures. At the same time, the emphasis on globalization and the importance of global learning for international businesses (Ghoshal 1987) has raised the issue of consistency among organizational structures within the cross-national corporation. The growing importance of internalization of competitive advantage as a requirement for cross-border success (Dunning 1992) and national bases for international competitiveness (Porter 1990) revive the basic question that the culture-free approach addressed: to what extent can firms facing similar contingencies (now found in a more tightly knit world economic system) alter their structures in new surroundings? The tension between a consistent worldwide structure and the demands of adapting to local conditions shifts the focus of the universalist question to the internal operations of firms operating across national boundaries. While this set of issues has given rise to a nascent 'neo-contingency framework' (Sorge 1991), neglect of the insights and tools of the culture-free approach continues. Why should that be so?

One answer may be that no one cares. The contingency approach to organization structuring seems to tell us little about behaviour in organizations that is of much practical use to managers trying to make sense of their worlds. To return to the example of the oil refinery, Gallie's detailed analysis of the same company's refinery operations in the UK and France led him to conclude that the 'evidence indicates the critical importance of the wider cultural and social patterns of specific societies for determining the nature of social interaction within the advanced sector' (Gallie 1978: 295). Is structure organization? This is a fundamental question, but one we feel should be explored carefully, particularly with respect to the level of organization and those behaviours we wish to make predictions about. Contingency theory and its cross-national applicability may have become too abstract in the researchers' quest to achieve the conflicting goals of a simple and generalizable theory which is also accurate (see Weick 1979).

The line of thought, first suggested by Child (1972), which explicitly recognizes a political/cultural/rational dimension to thinking about organization is, we think, more useful than supporters of the contingency view would have us believe. We propose that culture has a significant impact on the understanding of management and behaviour within organizations and is not just a residual explanatory variable. The convergence theorists' view that any cross-cultural variance in structures can be explained by the assertion that some organizations (in some cultures) have yet to catch up with contingencies in structural terms (Pugh 1989) does not stand up to examination.

CULTURE-BOUND THEORIES: HOFSTEDE AND FRIENDS

Culture-bound research has expanded greatly in the past decade and a half. In part, this is a response to the concerns of culture-free researchers, who have tended to focus on macro-level variables and structure–context relationships, rather than the behaviour of people within the organization (Child 1981). The conviction that the important aspects of cross-cultural understanding exist outside organizational structure were expressed by Axelsson *et al.*:

> Human preferences and decisions which are shaped by the values within society are refracted through individual personalities. Therefore, the organization and the behaviour of those associated with it must reflect the characteristics of the surrounding culture. There may be structural regularities across national cultures, but they are relatively unimportant in the face of the substantial differences in the ways that individuals interact and in the views they hold of the organization's place in its environment.
>
> (Axelsson *et al.* 1991: 68)

The move away from the culture-bound toward the culture-free approach was also spurred by the globalization of markets and businesses. Greater integration and more dynamic commercial environments meant that structures could not remain static, and individual cross-cultural interactions became more frequent and less constrained by bureaucratic guidelines. There was a need to understand the entirety of the organization, not just the structural features mandated by head office.

The study which has defined the culture-bound approach is Hofstede's *Culture's Consequences* (1980a). Hofstede's approach has had such an impact on the comparative field as a whole that few studies omit a reference to his work (Sondergaard 1994), and Redding (1994) has argued that his body of work provides a paradigm for comparative research. It has provoked praise and, of course, criticism; it has inspired replications and managerial usage in the form of taken-for-granted assumptions. We will discuss Hofstede's work as the key exemplar of this strand of research.

One of the most imposing features of Hofstede's original study (1980a) is its sheer scale. Data was generated from 116,000 questionnaires collected from IBM employees in over forty countries. Both the size of the sample and the geographic coverage were unprecedented. Since the respondents were all sales and service employees of a single company a number of factors could be controlled. All respondents were doing the same general task (selling and servicing IBM products) within the same overall framework. Thus the technology, job content and many formal procedures were the same. Only the nationalities of the subjects differed. Any variation in attitudes and values would, Hofstede claimed, be related to cultural differences rather than organizational ones.

Factor analysis of the responses to thirty-two questions about practices and attitudes revealed four underlying dimensions of culture. The first of the dimensions was *power distance*, an indicator of the extent to which a society accepts the unequal distribution of power in organizations. The second dimension, *uncertainty avoidance*, indicates the degree to which the members of a culture tolerate uncertainty or ambiguity. *Individualism* is the degree to which the culture emphasizes personal initiative and achievement rather than collective, group-centred concerns. The final dimension, which Hofstede calls *masculinity*, indicates the extent to which the dominant values in a society reflect tendencies toward assertiveness, the acquisition of money and property, and not caring for others.

Hofstede suggests that these four dimensions relate to the basic problems of humanity and 'are theoretically relevant' but 'they are not necessarily exhaustive; they do not represent the final word on dimensions of national culture' (Hofstede 1980a: 313). The dimensions, although treated separately, must be considered together as 'in the reality of each country situation the four dimensions interact with each other' (*ibid.*: 314). He later added a fifth dimension related to *time* (Hofstede and Bond 1988). The four original dimensions are statistically interrelated to varying degrees. Power distance and individualism are the most closely related (r = −0.67) (Hofstede 1980a: 316). Individualism and masculinity were not related at all for the forty countries in the original analysis.

Hofstede addresses the structural concerns of the culture-free theorists by relating two of his dimensions, power distance and uncertainty avoidance, to the structure of organizations. He argues that the interaction of the two dimensions influences organization structure and functioning. In cultures where power distance is high, power is the most important factor in maintaining the organization and protecting it from uncertainty. If power distance is low, there are two possibilities. Where people value adherence to rules (high uncertainty avoidance) a framework of clearly articulated rules can provide cohesion. In cultures where rules are not especially salient (low uncertainty avoidance) the organization relies more on ad hoc negotiation, which requires a larger tolerance for uncertainty (Hofstede 1980a: 319). The dimensions of power distance and uncertainty avoidance relate to the dimensions, or macro variables (see Starbuck 1981), of structure, isolated by the Aston group. Power distance is similar to concentration of authority (centralization), and uncertainty avoidance to structuring of activities. However, as Tayeb (1988) points out, Hofstede has little empirical evidence to support his interpretation, although he does cite some unpublished work on 'implicit models' of organizations that cultures hold in support of this proposition.

When Hofstede examined the four dimensions through cluster analysis he found that the forty countries could be grouped into eleven clusters at an error sum of squares of 12 per cent. However, these clusters do not appear to fit with his ideas of what they should contain. He explains this discrepancy by noting that the computer does not take history into account. He therefore regrouped the clusters into eight groups. Three countries, Italy, Yugoslavia and South Africa, are added to culture areas where they have an historic affinity. Japan is placed by itself as a unique culture (Hofstede 1980a: 332–5).

In addition to its scope, Hofstede's work is distinguished by including two separate surveys, one completed in 1968 and another in 1972. Although this is a relatively short space of time in which to observe changes in cultures, he uses the two waves of data to examine the *notion* of cultural change. In at least two of the dimensions, power distance and uncertainty avoidance, the questions comprising the indices do not shift together. Even where shifts do occur there are often a number of countries which shift in the opposite direction (Hofstede 1980a: 348–52).

His brief discussion of cultural change seems to undermine Hofstede's general approach. First, a shift of underlying values in only four years would call into question the stability of the culture as an influence on behaviour. Either the culture is not firmly anchored in particular values or the values were measured incorrectly. Second, Hofstede attributes some of these changes to technological advances. If this were the case, then we would indeed expect a convergence of national culture as innovations spread more quickly and completely around the globe. Hofstede finds instead that divergence according to his dimensions is generally increasing.

In his final chapter Hofstede (1980a) lays out many of the consequences of his findings for policy and future research. His main and unequivocal finding is that organizations are indeed culture-bound and that this 'applies not only to the behavior of people within organizations and to the functioning of the organization as a whole; even the theories developed to explain behavior in organizations reflect the national culture of their author, and so do the methods and techniques that are suggested for the management of organizations' (*ibid.*: 372). We think that he is right to challenge the universality of organization and organization theory, and, indeed, that societal norms may lead to 'particular political, organizational and intellectual structures and processes' and agree that 'these in turn lead to self-fulfilling prophecies in people's perceptions of reality' (*ibid.*: 373). It is difficult to understand how people from other cultures make sense of the world or arrive at decisions by applying a rationality that is not rooted in their own institutional frameworks.

Evaluation

How has Hofstede's work been received? If it is a significant contribution to the study of organization, how significant is it? Two linked review articles give us some idea. Goodstein concedes that there 'are important differences in national culture, and I have no important reasons to doubt that Hofstede's conceptual model does an adequate job of allowing these differences to be described'; however, 'that's as far as I'm willing to go' (Goodstein 1981: 51). In short, he rejects the notion that American theoretical imperialism exists.

Hunt, after describing Hofstede's work as 'one of the bright lights in an otherwise depressingly damp literature' (Hunt 1981: 55), considers some issues which Goodstein raised but did not discuss, including methodological issues and a potentially serious sampling problem.

There has been much formal and informal debate on the suitability of IBM employees as the target for his study, on the breakdown of the massive sample (116,000) into country samples, on the dominance of male responses (especially in countries where females are not found in executive positions), on the built-in bias of the sort of people (are they a minority?) who are attracted to and selected by IBM as employees, on the use of a survey to collect data and on the items from the survey used to establish the indices of difference. All these debates rest on valid questions.

(Hunt 1981: 55)

Indeed, after dealing with reactions rather than reservations Hunt concludes: 'His concentration on one multinational compels us to ask whether he is studying the culture of the Japanese or French or British or Malaysian executive or the culture of a multinational firm' (*ibid.*: 62).

Dorfman and Howell (1988) have documented some of the doubts that researchers have expressed about the validity and utility of the four dimensions at the individual level of analysis. They suggest that analysis at the individual level gives a very different picture from the ecological level of analysis used by Hofstede. They give the example of the 'correlations among the three items measuring Power Distance [which] are significant only at the national level, whereas the correlations among items at the individual level are virtually zero' (Dorfman and Howell 1988: 129). The difference in the strength of the relationships at the two levels is ascribed to Hofstede's use of average scores.

They also note that researchers have criticized the domain of items that measure the individual dimensions, and the labelling of them. The uncertainty-avoidance index is composed of three items 'which reflect seemingly disparate constructs: level of perceived stress, length of time the individual believes he/she will work for the present company and beliefs regarding whether rules should be broken' (Dorfman and Howell 1988: 130). They express the feeling that the scales are, in Robinson's words, a 'hodgepodge' of items 'few of which relate to the intended constructs' (Robinson 1983: 130).

There are also some statistical concerns addressed, due in part to the same item being included in more than one scale and some cross-loading of items on several factors. Of more concern is the level of analysis issue, in that the scales only measure national and not individual differences, and while some of these points are a bit esoteric for our present discussion they do indicate the overall flavour of unease prevalent in some quarters regarding the validity of Hofstede's work and findings. Hofstede has addressed some of these points, especially those concerned with the level of analysis (Hofstede 1991: 247–58; Hofstede *et al.* 1993).

Sondergaard (1994) took a more general perspective in assessing the importance of Hofstede's work by analysing the reviews, replications and uses of *Culture's Consequences*. He found that Hofstede's work was being applied in four ways:

1 Nominal quotations, mainly of the 'name-dropping' kind.
2 More substantial citations covering reviews and criticism. He only cites journal reviews and not the detailed kind of critique found in Dorfman and Howell.
3 Empirical use of the framework covering duplication and/or adjustment or application to different samples.
4 The final group accepted the Hofstede approach uncritically: 'In these cases Hofstede's concepts were used as a paradigm; a set of assumptions taken for granted. Hofstede's framework was applied in a speculative manner without any test or research based on the concepts' (Sondergaard 1994: 448).

Let's ignore the first category. The second includes commentators with contrasting views. On the one hand, there are a group of reviewers who praise the rigour, relevance and timeliness of the research; some of these point out constraints, while others bestow both praise and criticism (see, for example, Sorge 1983). Sondergaard summarized the three main strands of constraint as follows: were the data an artefact of the period studied? How did the fact that the respondents were from one company affect the results? Finally, is the use of 'attitude-survey questionnaires a valid base from which to infer values' (Sondergaard 1994: 449)? All three sets of questions appear to have some currency, but for us the crucial point is that the respondents came from the same organization. As Tayeb (1988) argues, how can we discuss the impact of cultures on organization structures if all the data comes from the same company? Are the respondents in some way different? Have they self-selected into working for this particular organization? Are they mavericks or in some way deviant with regard to the local social milieu?

Replications might help tease out answers to these questions. For example, Shackleton and Ali (1990), in a study of Sudanese, British and British of Pakistani extraction, found general support for the two dimensions that they used: power distance and uncertainty avoidance. When they plotted these on a graph they found that they were fairly close to where Hofstede's results would have predicted. They do, however, close with a familiar plea: 'What is needed now is an understanding of the implications of these cultural dimensions on specific organizational processes and facets' (Shackleton and Ali 1990: 117).

This latter point has exercised researchers from Child (1981) to the present day, although some authors who fall into Sondergaard's (1994) fourth category have made predictions or derived hypotheses taking the dimensions as given. For example, Axelsson *et al.* (1991) derived several hypotheses for a study on strategic decision-making behaviour in Swedish and British organizations using the concepts and positions of uncertainty avoidance and masculinity. Pugh *et al.* (1996), in a study of manufacturing organizations in Europe, set up and tested propositions on the use of coordination mechanisms using the uncertainty avoidance dimension. This use of Hofstede's work (see Table 2.6) seems to reflect the notion that his dimensions appear to make sense (Triandis 1994) and help researchers to make sense of culture, despite doubts about both methods and data source.

In a study which is a partial replication and extension of Hofstede's (1980a) work, Punnett and Withane (1990) reflect on the dilemma of continued use of the indices and instruments developed by Hofstede. They employed the four primary dimensions in a study of three diverse samples of respondents. They divided each group into two. The first study used a group of middle-level managers in a federal government department in Ottawa, Canada. The sample was split into two groups, Anglophones and Francophones, who worked in the same location, with the same tasks, at the same level. In this it came close to replicating the original IBM study. Punnett and Withane then developed a series of hypotheses on the general expectation that the Anglophone scores would be the same as those of the Canadians in the original study (Hofstede took largely Anglophone respondents) and the Francophone scores would be closer to the French scores.

Table 2.6 Representative studies utilizing Hofstede's dimensions

Issue	Study	Cultures examined	Findings
The utility of Hofstede's dimensions	Shackleton and Ali 1990	Great Britain, Pakistan, Sudan	Hofstede's dimensions were supported
Strategic decision-making	Axelsson *et al.* 1991	Great Britain, Sweden	The four dimensions explained some differences
The relationship of structures with Hofstede's dimensions	Pugh *et al.* 1996	France, Germany, Italy, the Netherlands, Spain, the United Kingdom	No relationship with structure; some influence on coordinating mechanisms
The reliability of Hofstede's dimensions in three settings	Punnet and Withane 1990	Canada, Italy, the United States	General support for the four dimensions

The second group consisted of American and Canadian fast-food managers in the Detroit-Windsor area (which straddles the border between Canada and the United States). While Americans and Canadians might be thought to be similar from the perspective of those outside North America, there are certain dissimilarities. Based on this, they again developed several hypotheses. The third group was composed of first- and second-generation North Americans of Italian descent working at the same level in the construction industry.

As a fairly crude test of replication studies, Sondergaard (1994) suggests differences should go in the same direction as the differences between groups in the original study. Using this idea, Punnett and Withane (1990) found support for twenty-one of their twenty-four hypotheses, although the actual level of scores was quite different from that of Hofstede. Their analysis of the rejected hypotheses, all from the first sample of government employees, suggested that there was a strong organizational influence on the scores.

One rejected hypothesis concerned uncertainty avoidance differences between Anglophones and Francophones. The hypothesis proposed that Anglophones would score lower than Francophones.

In fact the scores were the same. This suggests that the items making up this dimension might be related to organizational culture rather than a product of national culture (see Tayeb 1988 for a discussion of this issue).

Another rejected hypothesis also involved uncertainty avoidance, in that both Anglophones and Francophones were expected to score higher than in the IBM study but they were both much lower. Punnett and Withane propose that 'one might argue that the organizational culture of this particular government department encouraged acceptance of uncertainty rather than discouraging it' (Punnett and Withane 1990: 81).

Finally, they had predicted a higher power-distance score for this sample than in the IBM study but found it to be lower. Again, they suggest that if the organizational culture 'encourages the acceptance of uncertainty it might also support acceptance of equality' (Punnett and Withane 1990: 81). Overall, Punnett and Withane arrive at a conclusion similar to that of others who have utilized Hofstede's dimensions for explanatory purposes. The dimensions seem to have some predictive utility but their applicability may be considerably blunted by the intrusion of other levels of culture. They are thus hinting at an agenda which tries to disentangle and examine the different levels of culture, organization and nation. We turn our attention to this issue in Chapter 4.

THE THREE TRADITIONAL APPROACHES IN PERSPECTIVE

What conclusions can we draw from the above analysis of the naive comparative, culture-free and culture-bound ways of thinking and theorizing about comparative organizational behaviour? While each approach is subject to specific methodological problems, the underlying weakness lies in their theoretical bases. For the naive comparative approach, the lack of theory makes systematic accumulation of research results highly problematic. The culture-free approach utilizes clearly delineated contingency theory, but it may not be an appropriate base for examining cultural differences. For the culture-bound approach, the link between the dimensions which dominate such studies and the underlying theory is vague and contradictory. For us (and others, such as Tayeb 1988), the biggest problem lies in translating the dimensions of culture to organization.

What type of theoretical approach can help us to make predictions about differences in the behaviour of people within organizations?

We suspect that a different perspective on the impact of national culture is needed. Lammers and Hickson (1979b) have given us a start. They point out that 'the culture patterns prevailing in its social environment can affect an organization mainly in three ways' (*ibid.*: 403). First, governments and institutions can lay down procedures and rules which affect an organization's functioning, for example Companies Acts, Health and Safety legislation and taxation systems. This rule base arguably incorporates the norms and values of a society. In addition, values have an impact because organizations are located within a constituency of stakeholders. These groups are also thought to espouse the prevailing cultural values and apply them in evaluating the organization's effectiveness.

The second impact that culture has on organization is thought to result from its being embedded in the preferences and values of an organization's founders, and thus the design of the organization. This is an idea which has been further developed by Hofstede (1985) into the proposition that organizational culture is largely a product of the founder's culture. If we follow this line of reasoning, an organization in, say, Canada founded by expatriates from England is probably more British than Canadian. According to Lammers and Hickson, 'culture may affect organizational structure in as far as those who enact and shape organizational life have pre-existing notions about organization' (Lammers and Hickson 1979b: 403; cf. Child 1972).

The third way in which culture has an impact on organizational behaviour stems from the values of other participants, which may be different from and even in opposition to those of the dominant designers. To this extent, parts of the organization may be redesigned to fit more closely with the values of the people who occupy those roles or groups. So structure may be as emergent as it is deliberate. This tension may well be a reflection of, for example, the class structure of the society (Salaman 1978). This suggests a plurality of cultures, subcultures or counter-cultures operating within the social entity (or construction) that we call organization.

CONCLUSION

In this chapter we have examined in some detail the three traditional approaches to comparative organizational research outlined in

Chapter 1. We took key exemplars of these and critically examined their strengths, and in doing so exposed some of their limitations in theoretical, conceptual and methodological terms. Each of these has an impact on the utility of this research for those who wish to make sense of our multicultural organizational world, for those who must manage or work in cross-national teams, and for those who are responsible for working out strategies for competing across the borders of nation-states. It may also have an impact on those, at many levels within organizations, who have to implement or cope with strategy and strategic changes in various ways. These strategic moves may include technology transfer, joint ventures, mergers, acquisitions and direct investment.

We have argued in this chapter that even though many of the studies done under the three traditional approaches make sense there is little or no coherence to them. The findings of what we call the naive comparative approach vary enormously in both theoretical and methodological rigour. Research questions are quite vague and what focus they have is directed toward difference at the expense of possible similarities. The explanation for differences is both very simple and complex: variation is due to culture. There is, however, little indication of what culture is and, more significantly, how it works through into behaviour.

The culture-free approach is more theoretically grounded and the studies have more methodological rigour. For example, this approach to research often uses matched samples of respondents or organizations and subjects the data to sophisticated statistical analysis. It is, however, on the research question and the interpretation of subsequent analyses that this approach is found wanting. To put it simply, the focus of this kind of research is driven by looking for similarities; differences are explained away by vague references to national culture, late-developer effects or some other construction, without any specification of the link between culture and behaviour. Indeed, this approach is remarkable for its focus on organization structure to the almost complete exclusion of process. The theoretical underpinnings of the framework most commonly used have also been questioned. Is it too general to be useful or are its outputs too trivial to be taken seriously?

The culture-bound approach is certainly more theoretically sophisticated than the naive comparative, in that it attempts to investigate culture empirically. It is, however, weak in exploring the links between culture and behaviour. We suggest that it is also weak in both methodological and conceptual terms. The main part of our critique has focused on methodology and, despite some fairly sophisticated arguments (see Hofstede *et al.* 1993, for example), the main justification for the methods appears to be that the results make sense. For whom and for what purpose they make sense is not such an easy question to answer.

The second source of criticism is related to method but is really more conceptual. Are the constructs used to investigate culture themselves culturally specific? One of the early cross-national investigations of managerial behaviour used a value-systems approach (England 1975). How do constructs of values such as honesty, for example, translate across cultural boundaries? Are constructs derived from factor analysis or survey responses any less culturally conditioned? Are ideas such as human resource management and leadership culturally constructed? These are some of the questions to which we will turn in later chapters.

Overall, the three traditional approaches fail in that they provide no clear theoretical connection between culture – at whatever level it is measured – and behaviour. The lack of such a linkage inhibits theory-building and the constructive integration of research. It also means that managers in the international context can apply results only on a case by case basis. The field does not yet provide any general framework for analysing cross-cultural problems in a systematic way. In Chapter 3 we consider how these limitations affect macro-organizational issues in comparative management.

SELECTED READINGS

Hampden-Turner, C. and Trompenaars, A. (1993) *The Seven Cultures of Capitalism*, New York: Doubleday.

Hickson, D. J., McMillan, C. J., Azumi, K. and Horvath, D. (1979) 'Grounds for comparative organization theory: quicksands or hard core?', in C. J. Lammers and D. J. Hickson (eds) *Organizations Alike and Unlike*, London: Routledge & Kegan Paul.

Hofstede, G. (1980a) *Culture's Consequences: International Differences in Work-related Values*, Beverly Hills: Sage.

Kelley, L., Whatley, A. and Worthley, R. (1987) 'Assessing the effect of culture on managerial attitudes: a three-culture test', *Journal of International Business Studies* 18(2): 17–31.

Lammers, C. J. and Hickson, D. J. (1979b) 'Are organizations culture-bound?', in C. J. Lammers and D. J. Hickson (eds) *Organizations Alike and Unlike*, London: Routledge & Kegan Paul.

Lincoln, J., Hanada, M. and McBride, K. (1986) 'Organizational structures in Japanese and U.S. manufacturing', *Administrative Science Quarterly* 31: 338–64.

Punnett, B. J. and Withane, S. (1990) 'Hofstede's value survey module: to embrace or abandon?', *Advances in International Comparative Management* 5: 69–89.

Triandis, H. C. (1994) 'Cross-cultural industrial and organizational psychology', in H. C. Triandis, M. D. Dunnette and L. M. Hough (eds) *Handbook of Industrial and Organizational Psychology*, 2nd edn, vol. 4, Palo Alto, CA: Consulting Psychologists Press.

3 Strategy and culture

INTRODUCTION

In Chapter 1 we discussed some of the key issues in comparative organizational behaviour which confront managers and outlined some of the limitations that current approaches suffer in trying to provide answers to these problems. In Chapter 2 the three traditional approaches to comparative research were examined, specifically in relation to their theoretical base. While the three approaches offer different insights into the effect of culture on organizational behaviour, none of them provides a consistent guide to the increasingly integrated world that most managers – and many non-managerial employees – face.

Part of the problem with the traditional approaches is that they were generated in an era when strategic conditions were quite different. Long-range planning, five- and ten-year forecasts, and relatively stable corporate structures have now given way to more dynamic global strategies operating on short time horizons through more flexible, less formal structures. To open the discussion of a theory of comparative organizational behaviour we will examine changes in how the managers of organizations develop strategies to operate in a world largely unbounded by spatial and temporal horizons. We will examine how these developments have, in turn, led to changes in behaviour, and how culture influences strategic choices and strategic operations. This will serve as an introduction to a cognitively based theory of comparative organizational behaviour, to be outlined in Chapter 4.

Early attempts to understand the effects of international strategy were based on Chandler's (1962) work linking organizational structure to the effects of changes in strategy. Stopford and Wells (1972) utilized Chandler's framework to track the evolution of the relationship between strategy and structure in international firms. They attributed differences in structure to the degree of international commitment and the firm's emphasis on either product or geographical diversity. Galbraith and Nathanson (1979) focused more on growth strategies and how international expansion was accommodated in the corporate structure. From this point of view, the main task of senior management is structuring the organization to adapt to a realized strategy. Any difficulties posed by cultural differences are simply ignored.

At approximately the same time, an alternate view fuelled more by marketing considerations was emerging. If the corporation is viewed as having a set of production capacities and a stable of products available for world distribution, the basic strategic choice is how to allocate products to markets in order to optimize the use of manufacturing capacity. On the one hand, particular societies exhibit different tastes and styles, so that items need to be customized for local markets. On the other hand, manufacturing multiple varieties of goods lowers the efficiency of production and distribution. From this point of view, strategy resides in getting the correct balance between satisfying local needs and facilitating productive efficiency. Culture enters the equation through local variations in taste, style and consumption patterns, but not through any effect on management itself. Porter (1986) has offered a more sophisticated version of this approach, in which culture is reflected through the institutional arrangements of a society, mainly those concerned with industrial production.

This orthodox view, which is still to be found in texts on international management, was challenged by Levitt's (1983) pronouncements on the globalization of markets. He saw the globalization of markets and organizations as a potential source of enormous competitive advantage for companies. The major force for this drive seems to be the technology that has made the world a smaller place by revolutionizing communications, transport and travel. This has brought about a convergence in demand for consumer products as: 'almost everyone everywhere wants all the things they have heard about, seen or experienced via the new technologies' (Levitt 1983: 92). The increasing reach and sophistication of communication technologies and the rapid spread of technological developments has led to the emergence of global markets for standardized products and the rise of the global corporation. According to Levitt increasing globalization has made the world a simpler and not a more complicated place in which to compete. From the globalization perspective, a multinational view of the world and the associated multinational structure is decidedly passé. This form of organization operating in a number of countries, adjusting product, prices and practices in each, with the attendant high cost of control, will be or is being replaced by the global corporation selling worldwide product lines. There appear to be plenty of examples of firms operating in this way. Perhaps the most visible are of American origin: the two soft drinks giants, Coca-Cola and Pepsi, the fast-food chains and apparel companies.

This global view, while accepting that some differences in markets will persist, postulates that the majority will disappear due to converging consumer preferences. This, according to Levitt, leads 'inescapably to the standardization of products, manufacturing and the institutions of trade and commerce' (Levitt 1983: 93). It does not invalidate the general trend that Coca-Cola uses a slightly different product formulation for different markets, that it is possible to buy wine in Macdonald's' outlets in Paris, that Japanese consumer electronics manufacturers produce appliances for the various electric currents and voltages found in different parts of the world. The underlying product is basically the same and any distinction is only marginal.

Levitt tells us a good deal about strategy and focus in global markets but very little about the organization and management required to realize them. The basic assumptions behind these ideas have also been challenged. For example, Douglas and Wind (1987) provided us with an early critique of the standardized global product view and suggested that it was in fact overly simplistic. They view product standardization as being only one option among a range of possible product/market strategies that may be successful in global markets, and suggest that standardization may be appropriate only in markets which fit underlying assumptions or environmental conditions. They further conclude that a firm's international portfolio of products might contain a mix of both international and regional brands/products.

It seems that Levitt would have companies eschew market analysis based on cultural differences and proceed on the assumption that most regional differences are trivial or irrelevant. Strategy-makers should assume that the strength of similarities is more significant than any differences which may exist. In contrast, Douglas and Wind argue for a return to an analysis of consumers' preferences and tastes, while accepting that there are circumstances when a global product strategy might be an appropriate choice. The debate between Levitt and his critics is largely over how, and the degree to which, culture affects consumer choice. The impact on managerial efforts to realize the chosen strategy is not a concern.

Another approach to understanding international strategy can be found in the work of Killing (1983) and the Uppsala School (Johanson and Vahlne 1977, 1990), which developed a natural history of international expansion modes. Both approaches posit a sequence of involvement ranging from exporting to a target country to direct foreign investment. Firms and managers are seen as accumulating knowledge about a particular market as a necessary prerequisite for taking the next step of involvement. Culture is an important element here as it is manifested through local practices. Insufficient understanding of local tastes and techniques may undermine further commercial development. However, empirical tests of this model (T. A. R. Clark and Mallory 1995), while agreeing that learning about local markets does indeed occur, found that generalized organizational learning about how to expand inter-nationally occurs at the same time and results in new investments skipping whole steps in the incremental model. Thus firms would, in some cases, move from no involvement in a market to direct investment. This suggests that developing the general capability to compete internationally is more important than knowledge of specific markets.

The local-knowledge element found in the natural history school focuses on learning about a single country or society in order to facilitate operations there. In contrast, more recent formulations (Bartlett and Ghoshal 1987; Hamel *et al.* 1989) have emphasized the importance of obtaining knowledge from anywhere in the world and ensuring that it is communicated to whatever part of the organization needs it. Because these models are based on a global view of the corporation there has been less emphasis on specific cultures. In some ways this formulation simply adds the importance of global learning to the localization/efficiency trade-off, creating a three-way tension. Culture is again submerged, although it may appear as a source of advantages that can be utilized by other segments of the organization. At the same time, differences in culture may hinder the rapid dispersion of ideas through the corporation.

We should also take note of the trend away from thinking about strategy-making in purely product-market-analytic terms and the emergence of a resource-based view (Grant 1991), which focuses attention on the resources an organization possesses and the capabilities needed to derive advantage from those resources. One possible source of advantage might be a culturally specific marketing technique. Another might stem from the utilization of managerial talent from across the organization rather than relying mainly on parent-country sources, a policy that is linked to a geocentric mind set (Kobrin 1994). Both the resource-based view and the learning view are concerned with the global operations of the firm; this tends to bring cultural differences back into the equation, although at a lower level of interest than do some of the more traditional centrist approaches.

As can be seen in Table 3.1, theorists writing about international business strategy have normally considered culture only as it may affect local demand, and some approaches have even downplayed this factor. In virtually no case has the fact that the global organization must make use of a multicultural workforce to

Table 3.1 Approaches to international business strategy and their treatment of culture

Approach	Example	Treatment of culture
Strategy and structure	Stopford and Wells 1972	An indirect source of diversity
Economies of scale and local requirements	Porter 1986	A force for local adaptation; one of two main drivers for international strategy
Global markets	Levitt 1983	A declining factor
Natural history; Uppsala School	Johanson and Vahlne 1990	Cultural differences require local strategic adaptation
Global strategy	Bartlett and Ghoshal 1987	Cultural differences require organizational learning
Resource-based	Grant 1991	A potential source of competitive advantage

implement international strategies been considered. This does not mean, however, that there has been no study of the effects of culture on strategy realization. There is a body of literature which focuses on certain types of strategies and the way they may be affected by culture, as opposed to the factors which might affect the strategy itself. It is to this body of work that we now turn our attention.

STRATEGY FORMULATION

The influence of culture on strategy begins with its formulation. The formulation of strategy is composed of a number of steps, including scanning the environment for information, selecting relevant data and interpreting it, building a strategic model, testing it and putting it into action. Schneider argues that the steps in the strategy process are likely to be influenced by national culture: 'assessments of the environment and the organization are not necessarily "objective" but are a function of perceptions and interpretations which will, in turn, affect strategic behaviour' (Schneider 1989: 149). The approach taken to scanning the environment, for example, depends on what the strategist expects to encounter. While perceptions may be influenced by factors such as the history of the firm and the structure of the industry, the general tendencies of the surrounding culture are sure to condition the way an individual regards the environment. If the local culture embraces a proactive stance toward the environment, one that assumes the possibility of controlling it, the scanning may be more focused. More reactive cultures will take a wider, less specific view.

Schneider (1989) distinguishes between two general culturally influenced types of strategy. The first is a directive strategy. It is controlled by a small group at the top of the organization, and utilizes formal techniques for planning and evaluation. This approach is based on the conviction that the environment can be manipulated to accommodate the organization's strategy. The reactive approach involves more people throughout the organization, and relies more on qualitative information and informal evaluation procedures. Though Schneider does not say so explicitly, it seems likely that the directive approach would be more episodic, with planning for specific strategic tasks seen as discrete managerial decision cycles. For organizations embracing a reactive approach, strategic adjustment is more an ongoing task which links forward with the future and back with the past. Between these two general types there is room for an almost infinite variety of approaches.

While Schneider argues for the influence of culture on strategy-formation, she makes it clear that it is but one of many possible factors that shape strategic choice. However, it should be said that the point at which culture is likely to have the greatest impact is precisely where strategy is most fluid – during the scanning, selection and interpretation stages. While the threats and opportunities for the organization are still being formulated, the influence of culture on perception and cognition, on the process of recognizing and categorizing the issues that are likely to impact on the organization, is the greatest. Once the data has been gathered and evaluated, existing structures channel the process along more predictable lines, although these will also have been shaped by local values and practices.

The impact of culture on strategy can also be seen in its effect on the strategic decision-making process. Axelsson and his colleagues (1991) found specific differences between the behaviour of Swedish and British executives in making strategic decisions. The Swedish managers tended to take much longer to make decisions, to hold their opinions more strongly and to bring more pressure to bear on others in the decision arena. This implied a decision process which involved numerous intense interactions among those involved. These were informed by a larger number of experts, greater effort in searching for information and the use of more criteria to judge the decision outcome. With the possible exception of intense involvement, the Swedes seemed to employ a decision-making style which was similar to the more diffuse reactive approach described by Schneider. The British managers relied on fewer experts and more limited efforts in searching for information. One consequence of this was a speedier decision process. Axelsson *et al.* attribute these differences largely to culturally derived expectations about group decision processes.

In an earlier work, Drenth *et al.* (1979; see also Heller *et al.* 1988) focused on the influence on a variety of decisions of those at lower levels in the organization. The comparison of the Netherlands, the UK and Yugoslavia (as it was then) showed that Yugoslav workers, with their tradition of worker participation, had more influence on strategic decisions than their British or Dutch counterparts but that in all three countries top management had a disproportionate amount of both influence and rule-based power. Drenth and his colleagues attribute this difference, not to culture, but to the existence of the works council system that existed at that time. Nonetheless the differences may well reflect an acceptance of such arrangements or the expectation that a larger portion of the organization is included in the strategic decision-making process.

A group of Russian and American scholars compared decision-making processes in the US and the then USSR at the time of *perestroika* (P. R. Lawrence and Vlachoutsicos 1990). Much of their work focuses on the relationship between the socio-economic system and managerial operations. This relationship tends not to be quite so direct in the Russian case as is normally supposed. Soviet managers tended to rely more heavily on a hierarchically oriented, functionally specific system of management. At the same time, pressures for consultation with employees at lower levels introduced an element of grassroots participation which was at odds with more formalized structure and procedures. The authors suggest that the Soviet managers deal with these contradictory tendencies by alternating between the two approaches to decision-making. In both the Yugoslav and Russian cases it would be highly intriguing to revisit these findings in the light of subsequent developments. It would provide at least a partial test to differentiate between the effect of culture and the effect of a particular economic system on strategic decision-making.

A comparison of managers from China, Hong Kong and Canada by Tse *et al.* (1988) found differences both in the choices that managers made and in the processes by which they made them. The three cultures exhibited the most similar behaviour when the decision indicators were easily measurable (dropping an unprofitable product line) but diverged when the topic was less well defined (choosing between a standard or new product design). Again, the more ambiguity in the decision situation, the more likely it is that culture will play a role in the process of decision-making and the outcomes.

The importance of structure in the decision process can be seen in the roles of participants, as well as in the information and alternatives available. A study of the role of boards of directors in formulating strategy (Tricker 1994) examined the perceptions of Australian, Japanese and overseas Chinese of their roles as directors. Both the Chinese and Japanese directors saw boards as performing supportive functions for the top level managers, although in Japanese firms the function was more formal than operational. Both the Chinese and Japanese saw strategy in more abstract terms than Australian directors, who tended to view themselves as decision-makers more inclined to intervene directly in the strategic functions of the firm.

Finally, Ali (1989, 1993) has investigated the individual and organizational determinants of decision-making style for Arab executives. He argues that their decision-making styles have roots in the cultural elements of both Arab and Muslim experience. This leads to a preference for consultative and pseudo-consultative styles of decision-making within their own organizations (Ali 1993). Across Arab nations there are differences in the preferred decision-making style, due mainly to historical developments and outside cultural influences.

The process of decision-making, including strategic decision-making, is clearly influenced by cultural factors. The collection of information, its interpretation, the dynamics of the group making the decision and the contextual constraints under which decision-makers work are all influenced to a greater or lesser degree by the culture of those involved. The research reported above, like most comparative work, focuses mainly on the contrasts that can be seen between managers operating in their own countries. As yet we still have very little data on what occurs when managers move outside their local milieu or when they must operate in teams drawn from several cultures. The evidence that has been generated by investigations of international joint ventures (see the next section) indicates that strategic decision processes, including their implementation, may find conflicting cultural orientations a severe barrier to joint decision-making.

The effects of culture can be seen not only in the process of strategy formulation but also in the content of the resulting strategies, for example in foreign investors' preferred entry modes. A study of over 200 investments into the US (Kogut and Singh 1988) used a measurement of cultural distance based on Hofstede's four original dimensions to predict the type of investment preferred. Since managers generally prefer a lower level of uncertainty, it is argued, they will choose entry modes which provide greater control when cultural distance is high. Using regression analysis, Kogut and Singh found that both cultural distance and uncertainty avoidance affected the choice between a joint-venture and a greenfield investment. Culture is given a dual role here, influencing general preferences for a particular type of investment, and determining the distance between the home and the host culture.

In another examination of cultural effects, P. P. Li (1993) found that the content of strategy differed between firms in South Korea and Taiwan. These differences are attributed to, among other things, the values placed on family control of the strategic decision-making apparatus. This influences the process of decision-making as well as its outcomes. For example, reluctance to include outsiders in the decision process has limited options for growth strategies in Taiwan.

A more general study by Erramilli (1996) included American and European multinationals in the sample. In examinations of whether there were national preferences for majority v. minority ownership, cultural distance itself (measured using the technique employed by Kogut and Singh 1988) did not have a significant effect. However, increasing power distance and uncertainty avoidance were associated with an increasing tendency to favour majority-owned subsidiary operations. This effect remained even when the size of the home market and the size of the parent firm were controlled, although there was an interaction effect of size of parent and nationality on preferred ownership patterns. The studies of Erramilli and Kogut and Singh indicate that there is a net effect of national culture even when other characteristics of the national economy are taken into account.

In a more comprehensive examination of the factors affecting the location of US direct investment, Loree and Guisinger (1995) also found that cultural distance played an important role, although this role appeared to diminish as managers became more familiar with local requirements and practices (see also J. Li and Guisinger 1992). P. Clark and Mueller (1996) have also argued that culture is only one among a number of forces that may shape strategy preferences. In their view, organizations have room to manoeuvre with the national economic and cultural forces they face.

The fact that culture affects strategy-formation and preferences for certain types of strategy has received widespread support, but some authors have reservations about the importance of these effects, especially when they are separated from more general economic conditions. Hoffman and Hegarty (1989) examined nine European countries plus the United States for similarities in environmental scanning and strategic decision processes. While they found that nation did distinguish between some behaviours in the scanning and decision processes, the impact was small. The size of the firm was a better predictor than national identity. Moreover they found that the processes in all ten countries fitted the same regression equation, indicating that managers from the ten countries tended to use the same general model.

While the evidence supports the notion that culture affects both the strategic decision process and its outcomes, the effect of cultural differences on eventual success is mixed. Barkema *et al.* (1996) examined a large sample of foreign subsidiaries owned by Dutch firms. Those that were in countries with the largest cultural distance from the Netherlands were more likely to fail. Two studies – one by J. Li (1995), comparing Japanese affiliates in the US with those from other countries, and the other by Hennart *et al.* (1997), examining investments into the United States from Scandinavia and Japan – failed to support these findings. These studies and others like them may be inconclusive because two opposing forces operate between subsidiaries and parents. Increased cultural distance makes the communication and execution of strategies more difficult, but longer association promotes mutual learning, which can ease strategic tensions. It seems probable that cultural distance plays a part in the strategic role that foreign subsidiaries and affiliates play, but its effects may be submerged by other factors.

These studies indicate that both the process of strategic decision-making and its outcomes are influenced by culture. The summary provided in Table 3.2 indicates that, as Schneider (1989) suggests, culture can affect the process of strategy-formulation and implementation in a number of ways. The framework used to scan the environment, the role of formal decision structures, attitudes toward risk and ambiguity, and norms for the inclusion of organization members can all influence how a decision is taken. Culture can influence the strategic decision-making process at three levels. At the individual level, culture affects the attitudes and values of managers who make the decisions. At the organizational level, the structure of decision-making mechanisms, including the gathering and processing of information, will be culturally influenced. Finally, at the societal level, links between organizations and the larger economic and political apparatus will reflect cultural norms. The studies cited here provide some indication that cultural effects appear at all three levels, but their relative impact on strategy

Table 3.2 Representative studies of the effects of culture on strategy formulation

Issue	Study	Cultures examined	Findings
Strategic decision-making processes	Axelsson et al. 1991	The United Kingdom and Sweden	Differences in involvement, commitment, pace and information search
Worker influence on strategic decisions	Drenth et al. 1979	The United Kingdom, the Netherlands and Yugoslavia	Yugoslav workers have more influence over strategic decisions
Decision-making behaviour	Tse et al. 1988	Canada, China and Hong Kong	Decision behaviours and choices diverge when topics are vague
Decision-making style	Ali 1989	Middle Eastern countries	Arab and Muslim cultural elements affect decision style
Roles of boards of directors in formulating strategy	Tricker 1994	Australia, Japan and overseas Chinese	Australian boards are more likely to intervene; Japanese and Chinese boards are more supportive
The effect of cultural distance on types of foreign investment	Kogut and Singh 1988	A number of countries investing into the United States	Cultural distance affects choices between joint-venture and greenfield investments
The effect of cultural distance on mode of investment	Erramilli 1996	Several European countries and the United States	Power distance and uncertainty avoidance influence investment modes
The effect of cultural distance on affiliate survival	Barkema et al. 1996	Affiliates of Dutch firms	Cultural distance negatively affects the probability of affiliate survival

formulation, which is likely to change from society to society, is unclear.

JOINT VENTURES

When an organization seeks to enter a new market or to supply a current one it may seek a foreign partner to form a joint venture. The formation and operation of joint ventures offer several possibilities for the interaction of strategy and culture. First, companies from different nations may express differential preferences for the location of their joint ventures and the form that they take. For the most part, such preferences have been explained by using organization-level variables such as organization size, international strategy or transaction costs (Gray and Yan 1992). While there is relatively little comparative research on the topic of joint-venture choice, there is some evidence – both direct and indirect – that the decisions on which partner to choose and on the location of the joint venture itself may be linked to the values of the decision-makers and organizational characteristics which reflect the cultural milieu.

Many of the theories explaining the existence of joint ventures are based on a consideration of transaction costs. Under certain conditions firms may benefit more from internalizing their exchanges through a third unit in which each holds an interest. In one of the best known expositions of this approach, Buckley and Casson (1988) argue that both sides must resist the temptation to take advantage of the cooperative arrangement to gain a better strategic position if the enterprise is to be a continuing, mutual success. If the joint venture cuts across cultures, this may pose problems in a number of ways. The two partners may not have the same understanding of what mutual forbearance implies. In part this may be due to communication difficulties, but it may also be due to culturally influenced beliefs concerning loyalty to a foreign partner (as opposed to domestic industrial allies), the importance of fixed v. fluid agreements and the long-term strategic outlook of the partners. Where the perception of the agreement is rendered non-congruent by cultural biases the risk of accidental transgression of the mutual forbearance tenet is heightened.

One of the hurdles on which joint ventures may founder is perceptions of time. Several years after describing his four cultural dimensions Hofstede added a fifth dimension based in part on the perception of time (Hofstede and Bond 1988). Hofstede has said that he did not discover this dimension in his original research because there was little contrast in the way that Western societies perceived the action of time. It was only when parallel work was done in Asian countries that the distinction emerged. Contrasting time constructs and differing time horizons can have important effects on the operation of international joint ventures. Japanese firms are known for their strategies of long-term market penetration and growth, while American firms seek short-term profit maximization. In part, these contrasting strategies stem from different views of wealth accumulation, but they also have quite different time horizons. Contrasting views of time by dominant and minority partners in international joint ventures can alter the strategies themselves (Ganitsky and Watzke 1990). Dominant partners with longer time horizons may favour market protection strategies in their own milieu but market development strategies abroad. Chinese managers were more likely to trade time for accuracy when making a decision than their American counterparts (Baird *et al.* 1990). Where the view of time or time horizons differs between partners, as between Western and Asian or Latin countries, both operational and human resource difficulties are likely to arise.

Difficulties may also arise from basic conceptions of how the joint venture should operate. The Baird *et al.* (1990) study uncovered significant differences between the views of Chinese and US managers on the way that joint ventures should be run and the role that managers should play. Among other attributes, the managers differed on the use of authority and power, appropriate levels of uncertainty, and the preferred type of links between managers and subordinates. There was an especially pronounced difference on the subject of allocation of routine and important work. Such pronounced attitudinal differences do not necessarily mean that an international joint venture will fail, but they do mean that greater effort will be needed in order to understand and accommodate the partner's point of view.

Shane (1993) argues that a preference for high power distance in a culture denotes a lower level of trust. From this he hypothesizes that countries with higher power distance scores should prefer wholly owned subsidiaries over joint ventures as a means of foreign investment. Adding power distance to Contractor's (1990) market-based model for explaining preference for joint ventures over other types of investment produces a significant increase in explanatory power. Shane interprets this result as implying that higher transaction costs for firms located in high power distance cultures will cause them to prefer the more direct control mechanisms implicit in wholly owned subsidiaries. A similar argument has been made in relation to the preferred location of joint ventures. Because new ventures of any type create uncertainty, managers will seek situations in which uncertainty can be reduced or minimized. In cultural terms this means finding partners and locations with a small cultural distance from the investor.

The impact of cultural distance on joint ventures can be seen in the uncertainties that their managers encounter. In a study of role ambiguity faced by managers of international joint ventures, Shenkar and Zeira (1992) found that reported role ambiguity differed according to cultural distance. The authors used five indices of cultural difference, Hofstede's familiar four dimensions and a summary of the four which they labelled cultural distance. The composite measure was not significantly related to role ambiguity but the four individual dimensions were. As one might expect, perceived role ambiguity was higher when power distance and masculinity gaps were higher. However, higher role ambiguity was also related to smaller differences in collectivism and uncertainty avoidance. This would seem to imply that for some cultural dimensions being too close is likely to pose more problems than being reasonably distant. If two cultures have similar but not identical demands for uncertainty avoidance it may be difficult to know how much information is required before a subordinate feels confident in acting. If the difference were larger the problem would be better defined and the solution perhaps more obvious. The discovery of contrasting cultural effects among Hofstede's four dimensions also points to the dangers of simply summing a group of cultural measures and labelling the result cultural distance.

Within the international joint venture a good deal of attention has been paid to joint ventures between Japanese and Western firms, especially the causes of their high failure rates (Brown *et al.* 1989). While a number of explanations for failures have been offered, notably the mismanagement of the joint venture once it has been established, there are indications that some of the failures, at least, are due to cultural differences. One possible difficulty may lie in the very definition of success for a joint venture, or indeed any other enterprise (Turpin 1993). Japanese managers typically emphasize increased market share and the introduction of new products. For American managers, high return on investment and maximizing returns to shareholders are paramount. Cultural influences here may be expressed directly, through the criteria managers use to judge their own performance, and indirectly, through the mechanisms set up to manage the joint venture itself. The tendency for American–Japanese joint ventures in Japan to be headed by Japanese may ensure that short-term profitability will not be high on the list of priorities. This practice reflects a cultural preference for retaining prestige posts for nationals, as well as the practical considerations of local connections and language facility.

The difference in the objectives of Japanese and American partners is underlined by the factors that lead to Japanese satisfaction with joint-venture performance. Organizational learning, development of human resources and market diversification may all be factors which weigh heavily in the evaluation of joint-venture performance for Japanese participants. Japanese managers seem to recognize a wider variety of benefits that may flow from the joint venture, so their levels of satisfaction are not tied to a single indicator. This seems to be true for a variety of partners, not simply Americans (Cullen *et al.* 1995).

One of the key factors in the success or failure of an international joint venture is the management of human resources. Depending on the location, ownership and mission of the joint venture, there may be some ambiguity as to whether the unit's employees belong to the joint venture or to one of the parent firms. This ambiguity can be exacerbated by the time horizon of the joint venture and the value of loyalty to be found in the two cultures. The difficulty here may lie in the question not just of to whom the employee is loyal but of where that loyalty is directed. Japanese members who are loaned to a joint venture, especially one of short duration, maintain loyalty to the parent company in line with long-term employment prospects and the system of mentoring which facilitates advancement. Mexican employees limit their commitment to firms in part because of the strong collectivist attitudes centred on the family (Teagarden and von Glinow 1990). Failure to understand the framework in which partners evaluate loyalty and trust may lead to unrealistic expectations or failure to fulfil those of one's counterpart.

The success of an international joint venture depends on the fit of the partners. For most writers, the term fit refers to the congruence of strategic goals, organizational structures or personnel resources. For others, however, it has come to include the fit between cultures and its effect on human resource issues. A lack of congruence can affect organizational effectiveness.

> This lack of congruence would be any conceptual incongruity between the host and foreign HRM [human resource management] systems, for example, a highly specific selection system (or reward system, performance appraisal system or career path structure) versus a selection system that does not include assessment, recruitment devices and other mechanisms associated with highly specific systems.
>
> (Teagarden and von Glinow 1990: 27)

If the joint venture brings together cultures whose understanding of how employees are recruited, motivated and evaluated is at variance with each other the joint project will be severely handicapped.

The idea of fit or congruence can be applied to more general characteristics of joint ventures. Meschi and Roger (1994) examined fifty-one joint ventures between Hungarian firms and partners from five other countries. Using a perceptual measure of cultural distance, they found that greater national distance, as they termed it, led to significantly less organizational effort and organizational attachment, as well as higher levels of conflict. If the managers of the joint ventures perceived that Hungarian culture was distinct from that of their partners they tended to be less committed to the enterprise and to encounter more conflict over its direction. Although there was no direct measure of effectiveness, it seems safe to conclude that national distance does inhibit the effective functioning of joint ventures, at least in this particular cultural context. The distance between organizational cultures of partners was also examined as a factor affecting social effectiveness. While organizational culture also had an impact on effectiveness, in general it was less important than that of national culture.

International joint ventures represent an attempt by two or more cultures to work together toward some common goal. The research in this area, illustrated in Table 3.3, shows that culture plays a significant part in determining the shape of international joint ventures, the partners involved and, most importantly, their chances

Table 3.3 Representative studies of cultural effects on international joint ventures

Issue	Study	Cultures examined	Findings
Managerial roles in joint ventures	Baird *et al.* 1990	China, the United States	Differences in managerial philosophy and expected behaviour
Transaction costs and trust in international joint venture formation	Shane 1993	Several	Power distance helps explain preferences for joint ventures
Role ambiguity in joint ventures	Shenkar and Zeira 1992	Several	Cultural distance affects role ambiguity
Human resource context and joint-venture effectiveness	Teagarden and von Glinow 1990	International alliances in Mexico	Culture affects the employee relations of international alliances
Cultural distance and organizational commitment	Meschi and Roger 1994	Joint ventures in Hungary	Greater cultural distance decreases organizational commitment

of success. Precisely because the two cultures are brought into intimate contact the difficulties that may arise from operating with different cognitive frameworks are easier to recognize. Despite the evidence that culture is a crucial consideration in the design and operation of international joint ventures, there has been relatively little research directed towards understanding its actions (as opposed to its effects), perhaps because of the difficulty of matching theoretical concerns to appropriate methodological approaches (Parkhe 1993).

ACQUISITIONS

Although the strategic dynamics of international joint ventures differ from those of foreign acquisitions, many of the same cultural considerations affect both the acquisition process and its outcomes.

The steps leading to an acquisition are governed by five dimensions: time horizon of managers, involvement of top management, consensual versus individual decisions, understanding of competition, and analytical versus political decision-making (Haspeslagh and Jemison 1991). The first three of these are related to Hofstede's (1991) Confucian dynamism, power distance and individualism–collectivism dimensions, respectively. One need only consider the possible difference in time horizon for Chinese managers, which may stretch over decades, from that of Australians, which usually extends only to the next year end, to see how the acquisition process could be disrupted by culturally engendered misperceptions. To some extent, differing time horizons have been attributed to the structure of financial markets (Ghertman 1988), but the market structures are themselves influenced by a degree of social consensus around the appropriate term for investment maturation.

The understanding of competition is a more complex matter and is not easily reducible to a single cultural dimension. Managers may see the firm's competitive advantage as stemming from basic strengths within the firm, which may be functionally based, or as deriving from positions in certain markets. As indicated earlier in this chapter, international strategies themselves bear culturally distinct markings and many of these are driven by a specific understanding of competition. There may also be national differences in what is understood to be fair competition, as prescribed by law or common practice. For example, agreement among competing firms to hold prices to a certain standard is an indictable offence in the United States but common practice in other countries.

The acceptable limits of political behaviour within a corporation, Haspeslagh and Jemison's fifth dimension, differ widely across societies. The sometimes extreme political nature of the strategic decision process in Britain has been illustrated by a number of works (e.g. Pettigrew 1973; Hickson *et al.* 1986). In comparison with their Swedish counterparts, British decision-makers opt for a process dominated by a few individuals, with a larger set of managers maintaining a watching brief for their own interests (Axelsson *et al.* 1991). The Swedes rely on negotiation within a group with roughly equal influence to make strategic choices. When this type of difference is translated to the acquisition process, which often involves detailed negotiations between the buyer and the target firm, appropriate behaviour for arriving at a decision may delay or derail the process.

The importance of cultural fit has been investigated for mergers and acquisitions, though more often in terms of organizational than national culture. Where cultural fit is defined as attitude toward risk, decision-making approach, and preferred control and communication patterns, the lack of fit has led to lower post-acquisition performance (Datta 1991). The lack of cultural fit, or at least its perception by managers, also contributes to lower shareholder evaluations of the merged firms (Chatterjee *et al.* 1992), even where the firm exhibits cultural tolerance. Given that these studies focus on mergers and acquisitions involving firms from a single national culture, it would appear that the wider cultural differences to be found in transnational integrations would occasion similar strains but at a higher level of intensity.

While cultural distance may influence the degree of success in international acquisitions, there is some evidence that it may do so indirectly as well as directly. In a study of companies involved in cross-border acquisition in Italy, Morosini and Singh (1994) found no direct effect of uncertainty avoidance or individualism–collectivism on profitability or productivity. However, the interaction of each cultural dimension with the post-acquisition strategy adopted did show significant effects. Uncertainty avoidance in interaction with post-acquisition strategy showed an effect on profitability, while the individualism–collectivism interaction with strategy had an impact on productivity. For example, acquired firms from a country with higher uncertainty avoidance (such as Italy) showed better profitability post acquisition than those from a country with low uncertainty avoidance. For countries with low uncertainty avoidance (e.g. the UK or US), integration and restructuring strategies are more likely to lead to profitability. Matching an inappropriate strategy to a particular culture can seriously reduce the chances of executing the preferred strategy. This research is valuable for demonstrating a direct link between cultural fit and profitability, as well as illustrating the limits on post-acquisition strategies that culture may pose.

In a study which examined the integration mechanisms utilized in seventy-five international acquisitions in France and the UK, the authors found that the type of control exerted over the acquisition depended not only on the 'national administrative heritage' (Calori *et al.* 1994: 361) of the acquiring firm, but also on that of the company purchased. French firms tend to utilize more formal control in the integration process when compared to American firms, but less informal control. For acquisitions in France, the Americans were more likely to use formal procedures than were the British. It would seem that, at least in some instances, the importance of cultural distance plays a part in the strategies that managers use both to judge appropriate acquisition targets and to integrate them after the deal is closed.

As alternate international strategies, joint ventures and acquisitions pose contrasting issues for managers. Joint ventures generally have limited time horizons and limited objectives for both sides. The management issues involve the ownership of the project, the utilization of resources, including human resources, and the maintenance of a positive relationship between the partners. Acquisitions require the integration of the purchased unit into the firm, strategic reorientation and the eventual blending of two organizational cultures. Despite these differences culture affects strategic moves through the process of choosing a partner, through the negotiation of the attachment between the units involved and through agreement on (or imposition of) strategic ends. The effects (illustrated in Table 3.4) can be seen both in the structural arrangements made and in the success that they attain. There are clearly some fundamental considerations of cultural fit, often summarized in the idea of cultural distance, that affect both the content and outcome of international business strategy.

TECHNOLOGY TRANSFER

The cross-cultural transfer of technology faces difficulties that are more akin to those of joint ventures than those of mergers and acquisitions; indeed, many joint ventures are set up to facilitate the transfer of technology. The transfer of technology tends to have a shorter time horizon than other strategic options, implying that the interactions between partners rely on temporary structures of communication and coordination. The lack of continuing support is a common cause of failure in technology transfer operations, especially when the transfer is in terms of knowledge or technique rather than hardware. Because of the shorter time horizon and the lack of ongoing interorganizational arrangements, cultural differences

Table 3.4 Representative studies of cultural effects on mergers and acquisitions

Issue	Study	Cultures examined	Findings
Cultural fit and post-acquisition performance	Datta 1991	The United States	Differences in management styles lead to lower post-acquisition performance
Cultural fit and shareholder value	Chatterjee *et al.* 1992	The United States	Larger cultural differences lower the value gained in mergers
Cultural distance and post-acquisition success	Morosini and Singh 1994	Cross-border acquisitions involving Italian firms	The interaction of strategy and cultural distance affects post-acquisition performance
Types of control in post-acquisition integration	Calori *et al.* 1994	Cross-border acquisitions involving French and UK firms	The culture of both purchaser and acquisition affects integration mechanisms

which could be ameliorated over time can be fatal to a successful transfer.

Though there are few systematic studies of the effects of culture on transfer of technology, there is a general assumption that cultural distance may interact with other factors to influence the nature of the process and its outcomes. The level of industrialization affects the success of the transfer mainly through the ability of the recipient country to absorb the new technology. When the absorption capacity of one partner is low the gap between national cultures is likely to have a great deal of influence (Kedia and Bhagat 1988). The lack of structures, tools and attitudes to facilitate the acquisition of new technology means that the learning process must begin at a basic level, in terms of both the requisite base knowledge and the means for integrating new knowledge. Where both partners are at a high level of industrial development and used to incorporating new techniques, the issues of technology transfer are more likely to be strategic than cultural (*ibid.*). The major problems will arise in the negotiations over the conditions of transfer rather than during the process itself. While there is certainly some relationship between the level of industrial development and cultural values (Hofstede 1980a), the relative importance of the two for explaining the success or failure of technology transfer, or other strategic processes, has not been closely examined.

Hofstede's dimensions lend themselves to hypotheses concerning the impact of culture on technology transfer (Kedia and Bhagat 1988). For example, cultures with high scores on the uncertainty avoidance dimension may harbour a bias against any type of technology transfer, especially ones which cause a significant change in existing arrangements. Ironically, it may be easier to introduce a completely new technology into such a cultural climate than to modify existing arrangements. Similarly, where power distance is high, new technologies that threaten to undermine existing power structures, for example information technologies, may not be welcome. Organizations located in high-power-distance societies may also require that the transfer process includes upper-level personnel so that they can maintain their dominant position. Without their involvement and approval those further down the hierarchy may be reluctant to utilize the new tools. The efficacy of technology transfer may also be influenced by the interaction between overall cultural distance and specific cultural dimensions. A large cultural distance overall may amplify differences in attitudes toward individual achievement which might have gone unnoticed where the general cultural fit is closer. This consideration may be important for industrializing countries, such as India and Malaysia, which are beginning to export technology to countries which are less developed.

CONCLUSION: STRATEGY, CULTURE AND COGNITION

Formulating and executing strategy, more than other managerial functions, relies on the perceptions and judgements of the managers involved. Strategic decisions require that estimates are made about the future operations of markets, competitors, suppliers and regulators, as well as the reactions of employees to any necessary changes. The ambiguity of information and the limited definition of alternatives mean that biases and predilections, including those provided by national culture, may hold greater sway than in other, more structured functions. The greater scope for choice, the larger number of alternatives available to the global firm, also expands the arena for the operation of cultural influences.

The evidence outlined in this chapter indicates that cultural factors affect the process of strategic decision-making by making managers more or less open to various strategies, influencing their time horizons, limiting the geographic scope of their strategic vision, and even influencing the basic idea of how and where to compete. National culture may act directly on decision-makers, for example by setting limits on the degree of risk that they are willing to entertain. It may also act indirectly by influencing the perceptions that they carry of other, target, cultures. A manager in a large American multinational was asked by one of the authors why his firm did not have a subsidiary in Scandinavia, a logical choice given the firm's product line and customer base. The manager replied that the current chief executive officer (CEO) had once presided over a disastrous investment in Sweden which had temporarily checked his progress to the pinnacle of the firm. He attributed much of this failure to the attitudes of government bureaucrats in the host country. As long as he remained CEO there would be no investment in the Scandinavian region. The CEO's own cultural preference for low levels of government regulation interacted with his perception of Scandinavian culture as highly regulated to put one obvious set of strategic alternatives out of bounds.

One of the key factors influencing the success of international business strategy is cultural distance between the organizations involved. Studies such as those by Kogut and Singh (1988) and by Shenkar and Zeira (1992) imply that greater culture distance makes it more difficult for managers to work cooperatively on joint projects. While these studies provide important empirical support for this hypothesis, they do not yield much guidance as to what aspects of cultural distance are important or how these may vary by culture. It is not clear whether cultural distance decreases the probability of strategic success because it causes greater conflict, increases communication costs, lengthens the time needed to accomplish tasks or simply because it employs too much of the scarcest resource in international business, managerial expertise. Therefore managers do not know whether too great a cultural distance is a barrier which rules out certain strategic options or whether it means only that modifications have to be made to the strategic plan. Nor is it clear whether the relationship between cultural distance and strategic success is linear. It may be that there is an optimum cultural distance which would lead to respect for one's partners while still providing enough common ground for effective cooperation. After all, some of the most vicious wars of our era have been fought between ethnic groups who, on a worldwide cultural scale, are extremely close.

Determining the mechanisms by which cultural distance affects strategic success (or other organizational functions) is also complicated by inconsistency in both the conceptualization of the term and its operationalization. In some studies one or more of Hofstede's dimensions have been utilized to measure culture distance. Others have utilized more direct perceptual measures by asking participants how closely the cultures involved match on a series of factors. Both of these approaches are valid to some extent, but the lack of a more coherent approach makes the task of consolidating results on any but the most general level problematic.

In several of the studies cited above, Hofstede's dimensions, either individually or combined in an index of cultural distance, were used to differentiate between national cultures. The results indicate that in many cases the dimension approach provides a means of demonstrating that culture has important effects on strategy formulation, execution and outcome. However, focusing on only a limited number of dimensions does not generate adequate insight into how the perceptions of managers, which are key to under-standing strategic processes, are conditioned by culture. All international strategies, by definition, involve interaction between two or more cultures. When the interaction is relatively intense – as with joint ventures, mergers or acquisitions – the perceptions of those involved will set the initial conditions for success or failure. They will also interpret the evolving reality of the operation so that expectations are altered. Knowing that the cultures involved differ in power distance may provide a general guide to how the principles will interact, but it does not allow the managers involved to understand how salient this or any other dimension may be for their counterparts, or how it may interact with other factors in the situation. To acquire this type of insight we need to move beyond the dimensional view of national culture to one which more accurately reflects the framework used by individual managers in cross-national situations. It is to this set of cognitive problems that we turn our attention in the next chapter.

SELECTED READINGS

Axelsson, R., Cray, D., Mallory, G. R. and Wilson, D. C. (1991) 'Decision style in British and Swedish organizations: a comparative examination of strategic decision-making', *British Journal of Management* 2: 67–79.

Cullen, J. B., Johnson, J. L. and Sakano, T. (1995) 'Japanese and local partner commitment to IJVs: psychological consequences of outcomes and investments in the IJV relationship', *Journal of International Business Studies* 26: 91–115.

Erramilli, M. K. (1996) 'Nationality and subsidiary ownership patterns in multinational corporations', *Journal of International Business Studies* 27: 225–48.

Kedia, B. L. and Bhagat, R. S. (1988) 'Cultural constraints on transfer of technology across nations: implications for research in interantional and comparative management', *Academy of Management Review* 13: 559–71.

Morosini, P. and Singh, H. (1994) 'Post-cross-border acquisitions: implementing "National culture-compatible" Strategies to improve performance', *European Management Journal* 12: 390–400.

Schneider, S. C. (1989) 'Strategy formulation: the impact of national culture', *Organization Studies* 10: 149–68.

Shane, S.A. (1993) 'The effect of cultural differences in perceptions of transactions costs on national differences in the preference for international joint ventures', *Asia Pacific Journal of Management* 10: 57–69.

Shenkar, O. and Zeira, Y. (1992) 'Role conflict and role ambiguity of chief executive officers in international joint ventures', *Journal of International Business Studies* 23: 55–75.

4 Culture and cognition

INTRODUCTION

In Chapter 3 we examined studies which investigated how cultural factors influence macro organizational behaviours such as strategy formation, international joint ventures and acquisitions. While these studies illustrate interesting contrasts among various cultures, most suffer from two important limitations. First, most cross-national studies fail to identify the actual mechanism by which culture affects behaviour. The link with culture may be through the effect on individual actors, on company structures, on corporate policies, on the context of the organization or some combination of these factors. Without a clear model of cultural influence it is difficult to design studies which reach beyond the surface variations in behaviours to tap their underlying causes.

When comparative studies of macro organizational behaviour are considered as a whole, a second limitation emerges. Taken individually, comparative studies rarely extend beyond binational comparisons. There is occasionally some indication that the results of multiple studies might lead to an accumulation of results, but rarely is there any indication of integration across studies or across multiple cultures. Comparisons between French and British managers cannot easily be added to observations about their Japanese and American counterparts. Undoubtedly, one of the reasons for the enduring popularity of Hofstede's work (1980a, 1991) is that the ranking on four major dimensions allows comparisons among a large number of societies simultaneously. Integration of results is also complicated by the existence of differing research agendas and the use of varying methodologies.

Placing the quantitative results of international economists with the experimental findings of cross-cultural psychologists or qualitative work from the field of expatriate behaviour into any type of broad-based theoretical framework has thus far proved too complex a task.

The bulk of cross-cultural research has been carried out ostensibly to assist managers in corporations which operate across national boundaries; however, it is questionable how helpful it can be. The assumption of much of this research is that if managers from the parent firm can comprehend how those from other cultures act at home they can anticipate the foreigners' reactions and adjust their own behaviour accordingly. The implicit assumption is that corporate managers will encounter foreigners only in the foreigner's own culture. This is the logic behind the spate of 'how-to' tracts on dealing with other cultures that has recently emerged. Given the strong growth in international trade, increases in international mobility and communication, and especially the increasing integration of multicultural organizations, this basic model of the national at home covers only a small portion of the intercultural interactions that now occur.

As both Adler (1984) and Smith (1992) have pointed out, observations about how individuals interact with one another in their home country may not provide useful guidance for how the same people behave towards foreign visitors. Some cultures have very different norms for behaviour towards those who are defined as outsiders. Similarly, behaviour towards foreigners in a domestic setting may not necessarily be a good predictor of behaviour in other cultural environments. Both the context of the behaviour and the actor's own expectations may be quite different. Comparative research derived only from local experiences may provide a basis for understanding how individuals from a country behave towards each other but is unlikely to be specific enough to guide cross-cultural interactions, whether they take place in the home country or on foreign soil.

A similar omission can be seen in the application of comparative work to the functions of international managers. The assumption is made that understanding how a Brazilian manager, for example, operates in Brazil will furnish a guide as to how he/she will operate in a Dutch-based multinational. Such a direct inference does not take into account that the Brazilian manager will be operating in a context which is at least partially framed by the national culture of the Dutch parent. Since the home-country culture will influence the overall organizational culture there are at least three influences on the behaviour of the Brazilian manager: the home country culture, the host country culture, and the corporate or organizational culture. The importance of each cultural source will be influenced by the location of the interaction, whether at headquarters, within the subsidiary or at some other location in a third country. Hofstede *et al.* (1990), in one of the few studies to attack this issue, suggest that industrial and occupational cultures may also have an impact.

The barriers to generalizability found in most comparative studies have implications not only for conducting useful comparative research but for building a theory of international management. It is not enough to understand how actions, attitudes or norms differ from culture to culture. It is also necessary to comprehend how cultural factors act upon organizations, groups and individuals, and how those actions are affected by the contexts in which they occur. If the results provided by comparative studies do not focus on the mechanisms by which cultural tendencies are translated into action they lack a crucial element for building even a basic theoretical framework.

The emphasis on descriptive studies and the generalization of within-country behaviour to intercultural situations illustrate the limits of traditional approaches for generating a new theoretical framework. In order to interpret manifested behaviours accurately the personal framework within which the individual operates must be understood. Here, practical application and theoretical development require much the same agenda. For an active manager in the global context to function effectively with counterparts from numerous cultures he/she must be able to operationalize a series of linked concepts to analyse the construct–context interaction. This task involves investigating the various cognitive structures which intervene between national culture and the individual. In a typical international interaction this would include the cognitive framework of both participants and, by implication, that of the researcher as well (see Y. S. Lincoln and Guba 1985: 92–109). By understanding the information which triggers behaviour and the interpretive framework within which such triggers operate, one can attempt to project likely behaviour in another cultural setting. For example, if we can understand the cognitive structures an agent uses in cross-cultural negotiation we will probably be able to extend that knowledge to illuminate buyer–seller relationships. The cognitive framework through which an individual understands the world will persist, at least in the short term, even when he/she is faced with cues which do not easily fit into the available categories. Using a cognitive approach to understanding the cultural influences on behaviour, some of the underlying assumptions and frameworks can be made explicit. In this chapter we will begin to develop a model of how cognition mediates between national culture and individual behaviour.

The cognitive revolution has spread so widely that there is a large variety of perspectives from which to choose. For work in organizational behaviour, and specifically for the work presented in this volume, we incline more toward the interpretive, sense-making version articulated by Bruner (1990) and away from the computational, information-processing stream whose history has been outlined by Gardner (1985). Partly because the interpretive methodology has been more compatible with recent approaches to organizational behaviour and partly because of the level of specificity inherent in the computational approach, we feel the former is more appropriate for studies of comparative organizational behaviour at this stage in the development of this framework. The interpretive approach, through its links with anthropology and the role of cognition in understanding culture, provides a natural base on which to build a comparative model.

COGNITION IN ORGANIZATIONS

In Chapter 3 we argued that one of the ways that culture affects managerial behaviour is by shaping the perceptions of managers. All humans navigate through social settings by reacting to cues from others. In unfamiliar cultural contexts cues may be unclear or they may be interpreted in ways which are at odds with local constructs. Since Simon (1957) demonstrated the importance of perception in managerial decision-making, the question of how individuals perceive what is important in a situation has become a central issue in organization theory. Many of the approaches to this question have now been gathered under the general heading of cognitive theories of organizational behaviour, which emphasize the categories and frameworks that managers use to apprehend specific phenomena and to categorize them as familiar, similar to other phenomena or unknown. A good deal of emphasis has also been placed on the process by which individuals make sense of phenomena that do not fit easily into their existing frameworks (Weick 1979, 1995).

In a review article by Schneider and Angelmar (1993), studies of cognitive processes in organizations have been classified as research into cognitive structures, cognitive processes and cognitive styles. Cognitive structures refer to the way that knowledge is organized in categories, maps or other knowledge structures. Research on cognitive structures has focused on the categories into which information is habitually processed, the links that are made between different categories, especially causal links, and how these structures can provide short cuts in reacting to complex situations. Typically, individuals are asked to generate a number of factors that influence a specific behaviour or function, for example quality of performance or corporate strategy. The subjects then assess the importance of each factor and their causal interrelations. The resulting maps can be interpreted using both qualitative and quantitative techniques (Langfield-Smith and Wirth 1992). In a number of these studies there is considerable emphasis on the integration of shared cognitive structures among a group (e.g. Bougon *et al.* 1977; Walsh *et al.* 1988).

Cognitive processes include means of integrating and ordering knowledge through rationalization, simplification and sense-making. The question is not so much the content of the framework but the processes by which new information, especially that which is novel, can be accommodated. While research into cognitive structures has focused on the negotiation of shared cognitions among groups and their effects on facilitating collective action, much of the work into cognitive processes has investigated processes at the individual level. Decision-making and the way cognitive structures shape decision outcomes have been among the topics investigated under this category (e.g. Tverksy and Kahnemen 1974; Staw 1981). Not a few of these studies have dwelt on the negative consequences that may arise from adherence to an inappropriate cognitive framework.

Work on cognitive styles emphasizes dimensions of the cognitive framework, such as complexity or comprehensiveness, which affect cognitive processes. At the individual level investigators have focused on the capacity or preference of managers for certain types of information. At the group and organization level the reaction of information-processing structures to the environment have been interpreted as the key to operational success (Cray and Haines 1996). Overall, much of the cognitively based work has focused on understanding the components of the process, but some studies have related cognitive processes to particular aspects of managerial behaviour.

Since it is impossible to apprehend cognitive structures and processes directly, most of this research relies on the reports of subjects. Information may be elicited using a number of techniques; some of these rely on specific stimuli, while others take texts (both oral and written) as their raw material (Huff 1990). Because cognition is both reflected in and reflective of language, researchers have begun to pay more attention to the language employed by organizational members and to analyse its content (Laukkanen 1994). This development reflects the growing interest in the field in the importance of language and discourse in establishing and maintaining relationships in organizations (Drew and Heritage 1992). This means that the function of language, including the use of English as the language of international business, is the key to understanding cognitive processes in comparative research.

The basic thesis of a cognitive approach – implicit in much existing comparative research, although its consequences remain unrecognized – is that processing frameworks acquired in one culture persist and influence behaviour even though circumstances might change. The fundamental cross-cultural assumption is that a Portuguese manager who works in Portugal will act in accordance with a local outlook and that this is likely to cause difficulties when it meets with non-congruent or conflicting frameworks from another culture. What is missing is any understanding of the mechanisms used by the Portuguese manager in his/her own cultural space and the extent to which they may or may not be applicable in other settings. This approach has given rise to a literature which is bound by a static view of intercultural interaction, since cultural qualities are thought to be more or less permanent. A cognitive view recognizes the possibility, even the inevitability, of change as the framework is adapted to new circumstances. The outcomes of culturally specific cognitions are the substance of most cross-cultural research; analysis of the underlying processes by which they are created, and may eventually be modified, is generally missing.

Much of what has been written from a cognitive perspective focuses on processes of judgement. For example, Hogarth (1987) uses Simon's portrait of decision-makers with limited information-processing capabilities to discuss the ways in which we make sense of the world. He points out that:

1 Our perceptions of events and situations are selective, and 'anticipations' of our models of the world, our 'habitual domains', play a large part in what we actually do see. He goes on to suggest an interesting paradox: when we are confronted with too much information, we add even more in order to create understanding.

2 Integration of information is difficult and we tend to process it in a sequential manner. He suggests that this is not normally as serious as it first seems. It is only when there are major discontinuities in the source or pattern of information that this really becomes a problem. This may indeed be so if our maps are fairly accurate, but if they are not it may lead to the kind of pathologies which cause system failure (see Hall 1976 for an example).

3 People tend to use simple rules of thumb rather than exhaustive calculations as a basis for making judgements. These rules, stemming as they do from the experience of previous choices or from a desire to simplify, could also lead the decision-maker into traps.

4 As humans have limited memory capacity, we tend to use associations to reconstruct past events.

One of the most important tools for research into cognitive structures is the cognitive map (Fiol and Huff 1992). Cognitive mapping is a technique which attempts to elicit the relationships that the individual has with different elements in the environment (Eden 1992). The focus is not on the categories in which the manager places items, but on the relationships between those categories. The sample cognitive map in Figure 4.1 illustrates how a subsidiary manager might view the elements in a subsidiary's strategic environment. One of the advantages of using the cognitive-mapping approach is that it links the individual elements in the cognitive structure to the whole (Fletcher and Huff 1990). There are numerous types of maps and mapping techniques: they may focus on the categories that individuals perceive, on the associations among the categories or on the causal links that exist in the knowledge structure (Huff 1990).

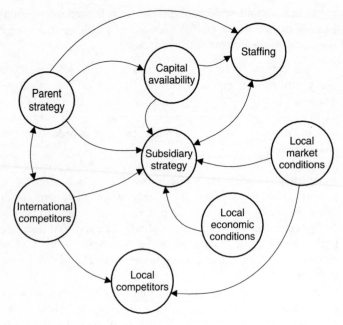

Figure 4.1 Example of a cognitive map

While cognitive-mapping techniques tend to focus on the links among relatively fixed categories of knowledge structures that managers use, sense-making emphasizes the integration of information that cannot immediately be assimilated into existing frameworks.

In the loosely coupled, chaotic, anarchic world of the organization, differences are everywhere and people need abstractions to smooth over the differences. People also need to become cartographers in order to fashion those disconnected abstractions into plausible patterns.

(Weick 1990: 8)

Managers need not only to be able to map their territories but also to bring in and develop different maps or models to use in novel situations. This means that they need to be able to modify and correct their maps when the patterns do not explain a new situation. The failure of sense-making mechanisms may lead to inappropriate actions which can have severe consequences (Weick 1988, 1993).

Another approach to understanding cognitive processes is the notion of scripts. A script (Gioia 1986, 1992) is a sequence of events or actions, usually with a temporal order, which are salient for an actor because the script has proved useful in dealing with recurring situations. A script provides a ready response to familiar situations and thus represents a short cut for the use of accumulated experience and wisdom. Scripts also put limits on the ways in which managers may respond if the situation is unusual, unprecedented or mistakenly matched with an inappropriate script. Storytelling may be used to work out scripts which incorporate past events and anticipate future developments. Variations of a story may be tested through repetition among a group until a script is negotiated which is acceptable to all concerned.

An incident which happened to one of the authors, who lives in Canada, may provide an illustration of how scripts can hold a culturally specific content. The author was interviewing the head of a British firm and was invited to lunch. They were joined in the executive dining room by another dozen or so managers from the firm. The main topic of conversation was a series of important matches between the English and Australian cricket teams which had begun that morning. By chance, the Canadian had attended an earlier match between the Australians and a county team, a warm-up for the current series. He therefore gave a brief summary of what he had seen and his impressions of the various players and their capabilities. The effect was impressive. There was a short but universal silence and then the talk turned to other topics. Clearly the Canadian had failed to fit in with a social script designed to enlighten the bewildered foreigner, which called for detailed descriptions of cricket as both a game and a social event (a script that appears to be available to all Britons whether or not they have any interest in cricket). For most of those in the room, there simply was no category for 'Canadian knowledgeable about cricket'. What sense-making techniques were used after his departure is unknown.

The essence of all these techniques for analysing cognitive behaviour lies in understanding how individuals and groups interpret their immediate environment. Distinct mental categories, differing links between categories, and negotiated understandings about cause and effect relationships form the perceptions which allow individuals and groups to act. Differences in perception form the implicit basis for comparative research. It clearly is not enough to observe that behaviours differ across cultures; we must be able to understand how those differences come into being. The consequences of cross-cultural behaviour lie not only in inappropriate or misunderstood actions, but also in the changes that the interpretation of these causes in cognitive frameworks. The conceptual framework of comparative management needs to be expanded by the inclusion of cognitive elements.

A MODEL OF CULTURAL EFFECTS ON BEHAVIOUR MODIFIED BY COGNITION

The basic assertion in most cross-cultural research is that national culture, usually expressed in terms of values or beliefs held by the majority of a nation's members, has a direct impact on individual behaviour. As indicated in Figure 4.2, no factors are normally specified which transmit or modify the aggregate tendencies found at the societal level to the actions observed at the individual level.

There are two major difficulties with this model. First, the relationship between values and behaviour is notoriously weak. Even in controlled experimental settings the number of other factors that may intrude is quite large. When one is operating with a generalized tendency across a large population in which the individual exists in several levels of culture (Trompenaars 1993) the possibility of accurate predictions becomes very small. Second, applications of this model usually have little, if anything, to say about how the values embedded in the national culture and taken on board by the individual influence behaviour. Since values held by the individual may lead to contradictory impulses, or similar impulses may manifest themselves in contrasting actions, this leaves both the analyst and the manager who must deal with someone from another culture somewhat in the dark.

By interposing the cognitive framework of the individual between national culture and behaviour in the model, the link between the values held under national culture and the key individual behaviours that are exhibited can be better understood. If one can determine the

national culture ————————▶ behaviour

Figure 4.2 Basic cultural model

categories by which managers comprehend their environment the available behaviours are clarified and the link between stimulus and behaviour is elucidated. This is true not only for situations which are or appear to be familiar, but also for those for which the cognitive framework offers no readily available categories. Through the concepts of sense-making, one can understand how individuals seek to integrate new data that do not fit easily into existing structures. Analysing the cognitive framework consists not merely in specifying the nodes and links in the cognitive map but also in understanding how the map itself is reproduced and modified. With these mechanisms it becomes clearer which values may be triggered and applied in the choice situation.

As an example of the process captured in Figure 4.3, consider the case of a local manager in Malawi. Mr Mwase, as we will call him, is a Malawian national who works for an international company with its headquarters in Britain. As part of his duties he must appoint someone to a junior accounting post in the subsidiary. From the point of view of his employers, he should hire someone who is technically competent, even though the person hired will be given substantial training. If the clerk was being hired in the United Kingdom by a British manager the categories of technical competence, education and the promise of future development would likely be the most important. There are a number of candidates who fulfil these requirements. Some are graduates of the local business school, while others are employees of domestic firms. While job-related factors are important in the Malawian context, Mr Mwase must also give strong consideration to family connections, though not necessarily to his own family as he is too junior in the firm to use his influence in this way. His immediate superior has two cousins (the term is rather encompassing) who meet the minimum qualifications for the job. The nationality of the applicants is another important category because of government regulations which

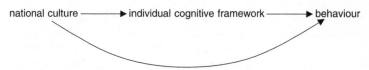

Figure 4.3 Individual cognition as an intervening variable

severely limit the possibility of hiring foreigners. This is relevant because another, non-family, applicant is a long-time resident who works for a competing foreign firm.

This vignette provides an opportunity to compare the cognitive approach with the traditional approaches discussed in Chapter 2. Under the naive comparative approach the research could only assert that there is a difference in personnel practices between Malawi and Britain. For a researcher utilizing a culture-free approach, the similarities in the allocation of authority for making personnel decisions would be the important issue, not the characteristics of those who might be chosen. Using the culture-bound model one would be able to say that the local values influenced the choice that the manager made but not how values were connected to behaviour. If we adopt a cognitive approach we can examine the categories that are important for the hiring manager in this situation and how they differ from those in another cultural context. Since he will have encountered similar situations before, the Malawian manager would have little trouble in categorizing the hiring possibilities and their interconnections. Being able to tap those cognitions would allow the researcher both to connect them more clearly to particular values and, what may be more important, to understand how a similar problem might be understood in other contexts. If the manager was to be promoted to a regional headquarters it is likely that the same categorization would occur to him if he were required to hire.

This example raises another issue concerning the proposed model. One of the influences on the Malawian manager would be the culture of the organization in which he works. The contending demands of the hiring process would have been encountered before by others in the organization and solutions would have been adopted, presumably in accord with the organizational culture. If the parent company emphasizes the need for close understanding and attention to outside social obligations it is likely that more consideration of kinship ties will be important. If technical competence and the Western tendency towards emphasizing individual merit over collective claims are more important these will loom larger in the hiring decision. Organizational culture will influence behaviour directly, for example by the operation of groups norms, and through its effect on the cognitive framework. Organizational culture will itself be influenced by the larger culture, and thus intervene between the national culture and individual cognition, as illustrated in Figure 4.4.

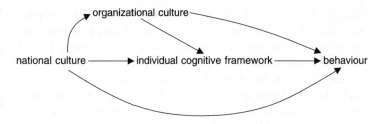

Figure 4.4 Adding organizational culture to the model

Notice that the model allows for national culture to affect the cognitive framework either directly or through its effect on organizational culture. This raises the question of whether the direct and indirect effects are necessarily consistent. It seems possible that, while some consistency would be required, the manifestation of a given value in an organization would lead to actions which, if not contradictory to the original value, would have divergent implications. In the example above, the firm as a whole might set great store by the application of universal criteria for hiring and promotion. In that case the overall organizational culture, though perhaps not that of the local subsidiary, would embrace values that were incompatible with the national culture in which the subsidiary was located.

The relationship between national culture and organizational culture is one that has not received much attention in the literature, although Wong-Rieger and Rieger (1989) provide an interesting example. For the most part, those who are interested in organizational culture have neglected the effects of larger cultural contexts (Alvesson 1993: 78–81). Since the possibility of links between levels of culture has been neglected there has been little consideration of possible cross-level influences.

The neglect of the relationship between organizational and national culture is ironic. Japan's burgeoning economic success in the late 1970s and early 1980s, and the concomitant decline of American economic dominance, led to a search for concept which would help to explain the obvious differences in productivity and commercial success between the two countries (Meek 1988). Ouchi (1981) traced these organizational differences to their roots in their respective national cultures and argued that some features of Japanese management, especially related to human resource strategies, could be adapted to Western, more particularly American, firms. For Ouchi, the link between national and organizational culture was crucial. When these insights were popularized by the Excellence Movement (Peters and Waterman 1982; Deal and Kennedy 1982) the link between national and organizational culture was neglected. Organizational culture was seen as an organizational attribute or managerial function which could be created and manipulated with little regard for its surrounding context. The success of this approach, at least from the consultants' point of view, led to the conceptual and analytical divorce of national and organizational culture almost before the marriage had been performed.

One of the few studies to address directly the relationship between culture at the national and organizational levels was conducted by Hofstede *et al.* (1990). They argue that national culture and organizational culture flow from different sources. National culture, in their view, consists of a more diffuse set of orientations which arise mainly from basic values inculcated early in life through the family and by other socialization mechanisms that operate during early childhood. Though values play a role at the organizational level, culture there is based more on specific work practices which are acquired within the organization, especially through additional later socialization processes. Hofstede *et al.* also postulate an intervening level of culture, the occupational level, which is influenced equally by values and practices.

Using methodology similar to that found in *Culture's Consequences*, the researchers attempted to extract the underlying dimensions of organizational culture from a sample of twenty units in ten organizations across two countries, Denmark and the Netherlands. Their results (reported in Hofstede *et al.* 1990; Hofstede 1991) describe six dimensions which underlie organizational culture. They are process- versus results-oriented, employee- versus job-oriented, parochial versus professional, open versus closed system, loose versus tight control and normative versus pragmatic. The content of these dimensions is not particularly surprising as they have all been discussed, in some fashion, in earlier work in the field.

What is more interesting is that their measures of values, many of which are the same as those used in the earlier cross-national study (see Chapter 2), do not explain much variance across organizations, although the results are significant. The dimensions derived from work practices are much more powerful in distinguishing among the twenty organizations than national values. It is not clear, however, whether work practices are useful in distinguishing between the two countries involved in the study. Hofstede and his colleagues (1990) interpret these findings to mean that national culture is based on the more abstract and diffuse collection of sentiments to be found in values, while organizational culture is defined by work practices which are acquired later in life and which have more immediate connections with specific organizational functions. They see little connection between work practices and national values.

While there are a number of methodological issues embedded in this work (see Hofstede *et al.* 1993 for a partial discussion) which make interpretations of their findings difficult, this study does begin to address empirically the relationship between national and organizational culture. The authors conclude that national culture may have some effect on organizational culture, but that it is muted and likely to influence only certain sectors. However, this conclusion is not tested directly. Even though the researchers have parallel data on values and work practices for each unit, only the differences in values at each level are discussed in terms of national comparisons. Practices and values are factor-analysed separately to extract underlying dimensions, but a statistical analysis of the comparative power of values and practices is not provided. A combined analysis might have found that some factors would draw on both values and practices to distinguish among organizations. The key question – the comparative importance of national and organizational culture for understanding organizational behaviour – is not addressed. The two concepts are kept distinct theoretically and empirically.

While the results of Hofstede's group point to a separation of national and organizational culture, it seems probable that some relationship between the two does exist. Several students of organizational culture (e.g. Beck and Moore 1985; Meyerson and Martin 1987) have pointed to the 'complicated embeddedness of organizational cultures' (Alvesson 1993: 79–80). Trompenaars proposes that four prototypical organizational cultures can be generated by crossing the cultural dimension of equality v. hierarchy with that of task v. person orientation (Trompenaars 1993: 138–63). This generates four types of organizational cultures: the family, the rocket, the Eiffel Tower and the incubator. Every culture – in this case equated with a country – has a stronger or weaker affinity with one of these types. Spain, for example, is likely to have organizations with a family culture while Germans favour the Eiffel Tower type. The influence links between the levels of culture are quite vague in Trompenaars' formulation, but there is some empirical support for their existence.

One possible link is the effect that founders and leaders have on organizational culture (Schein 1983; Gagliardi 1986). Since founders presumably participate in the national culture there must be some flow-through from the values underlying national culture to those exemplified by the founder. Even Hofstede's argument that organizational culture rests on a distinct task-related basis leaves unanswered the question of what the content of that basis is. Surely work-related practices must in some way be linked to national culture. Hofstede has stated in a number of his works that IBM, the source of data for his monumental work, has a singular organizational culture. While this must to some degree be true, it is not the same as saying that all the various subsidiaries in the IBM fold had identical organizational cultures. The culture of each subsidiary must be a mix of the overall corporate culture (in part derived from the American national culture) and the national culture surrounding the subsidiary. Given the lack of research into how subsidiary cultures may vary, the link between organizational and national culture and the effect of this relationship on behaviour must remain an intriguing and important empirical issue.

The model, shown in Figure 4.4, postulates a direct relationship of both national and organizational culture with behaviour. It also indicates that both types of culture will have an impact on behaviour through the cognitive processes and structures employed by the individuals in the organization. There is another, somewhat controversial, element that may intervene between national culture and behaviour, that of organizational cognition.

There has been a considerable debate over whether or not congnition exists at the organizational level. It is argued that only individuals can apprehend phenomena, categorize and utilize information. The results of cognition may be passed on to others, but the act of cognition itself cannot be shared (Glick 1985; James *et al.* 1988). Against this view are ranged those who believe that organizations depend on cognitive views or maps shared by at least some of the organization's members (Langfield-Smith 1992;

Schneider and Angelmar 1993; Laukkanen 1994). Without shared cognition, they argue, the link between apprehension and action would have to be continually renegotiated. This implies not that all members of the organization must have the same set of cognitions, but that for those who share certain responsibilities, especially decision-making duties, some degree of congruence among cognitive frameworks must exist.

It might also be argued that an organizational cognitive framework is really only a subset of organizational culture, that the proposed model would be more parsimonious if the organizational cognitive framework was subsumed under the organizational culture concept. While there is a possible overlap between the two concepts (and some authors appear to believe that they are equivalent), we believe that examining the organizational cognitive framework separately helps to clarify its status as a set of shared categories through which groups negotiate and maintain common perceptions of their environment. Organizational culture may be expressed in a wide variety of ways, including through values, beliefs, symbols, myths and ceremonies. This diversity may result, not in a unitary, clear perception of organizational culture, but in one which is rooted in ambiguity and uncertainty (Martin and Meyerson 1988). Organizational cognition, on the other hand, requires that cognition, at least to some extent, is shared. It is a more specific and more limited concept than organizational culture, and one that links the underlying construct more directly with behaviour. The existence of organizational culture does not, in our view, presuppose organizational cognition, much less clarify the strength of shared perceptions.

The addition of the organizational level of cognition to the model (shown in Figure 4.5) enhances it in several ways. First, it makes explicit the need for overlapping cognitive frameworks among those working together in a unit. This is an important issue when individuals of two or more nationalities are working together. The classic case occurs when a subsidiary is headed by a home-country national and staffed by host-country nationals. Without a shared cognitive framework, communication and effective action become much more problematic. More recently the integration of multi-national research and development (R&D) teams provides an arena in which a shared cognitive map is crucial for the rapid and efficient completion of tasks. This is a case where there may be little in the way of shared culture, organizational or otherwise, but there is a

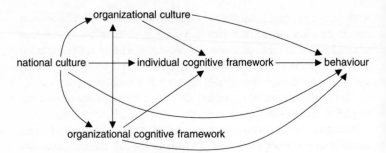

Figure 4.5 The cognitive model

high level of shared perceptions, at least as far as the task at hand is concerned.

Examining common cognitive patterns also helps us to disaggregate the effects of organizational culture and national culture on individual behaviour. Organizational culture affects behaviour directly by providing guidelines and expectations for organizational members. If, for example, corporate loyalty is an important value in the organizational culture, then individuals may be expected to make positive statements and refrain from negative assessments, at least outside the organization. Eventually this may lead an employee to make loyal–disloyal an important category in assessing potential statements. Finally, the group may develop a common understanding of which behaviours are important for demonstrating company loyalty and which must be avoided. Thus organizational culture can act on individual behaviour directly, or indirectly through its effect on cognitive frameworks at the individual and organizational level.

A similar statement may be made about the link between national culture and the individual cognitive framework. The categories and connections utilized by an individual can be affected directly, by national culture, or indirectly, through the effect of national culture on organizational culture or a shared cognitive framework. For example, in a culture where personal loyalty to the leaders of the organization is important this value may affect an employee's evaluation of external employment opportunities through direct reference to the loyalty one choice or the other might demonstrate. Equally, the employee may already have categorized similar choices as being loyal, disloyal or neutral, or the group may have negotiated a series of scripts incorporating the loyalty dimension. All three levels may influence the eventual choice. The degree to which national culture, the individual's cognitive framework and group cognitive processes operate will depend on a number of factors, including the salient features of the national culture itself.

The cognitive model of behaviour presented in Figure 4.5 should not be considered exhaustive. We do not mean to imply that we have considered all the relevant variables which may influence individual behaviour or all the possible connections among the variables presented. There is, for example, no explicit consideration of factors such as organizational structure or economic system in the model. Nor do we introduce the numerous other individual attributes, such as personality factors, job tenure or position in the organization, which will affect both individual cognitive frameworks and behaviour. Finally, the relationships in the model could be expanded to include feedback loops such as the possible effect of individual behaviour on the individual cognitive framework. This loop would be especially important when examining the behaviour of expatriates encountering a new culture. As their behaviours are seen to be inappropriate or ineffective the cognitive framework will have to be altered. Failure to alter it may lead to culture shock or withdrawal.

The model is intended to illustrate the importance of cognition for understanding, and more importantly comparing, behaviours across cultural boundaries. By focusing on cognitive structures, processes and styles, and their components, the model promotes better understanding of why contrasting behaviours occur, rather than simply focusing on the differences in behaviours. The inclusion of organizational-level cognition and its relation to national and organizational culture allows researchers and managers to differentiate between cognitive components which are affected by deep-seated influences, such as national culture, that are unlikely to be changed, and those which may be more amenable to manipulation. The linkage between the two levels of culture and the two levels of cognition holds out some hope of developing a theoretical basis for a multinational rather than binational understanding of cross-cultural differences. Finally, the model focuses on the links from the societal and organizational levels to individual behaviour. Instead of assuming, as all three traditional approaches do, that the intervening levels are irrelevant, the model highlights the various paths by which national culture may affect individual behaviour.

One of the few comparative studies which adopts a cognitive point of view is an examination of cognitive maps for managers in four industries carried out by Calori *et al.* (1992). A single informant from each of seventeen French and sixteen British companies was interviewed to construct a cognitive map showing the competitive forces in the firm's environment. Although they did not set out to test cross-cultural effects the authors found that the frames of reference for the managers in the two countries differed in important ways. At the aggregate level, the managers indicated significant differences in both their view of the structure of the commercial environment and their perceptions of the environment's dynamics. For example, French executives were more attuned to differences between large and small companies, segmentation of the market and the distinction between distribution channels. The authors argue that this reflects the 'Cartesian, rationalistic nature of their educational system and culture' (Calori *et al.* 1992: 72). The British managers tended to be more cognizant of the government's role, especially in terms of anti-trust legislation, and the importance of profit and shareholder value.

The French and British managers could also be distinguished by the way they viewed the dynamics of their industries. The British exhibited a shorter time horizon, at least for profitability, than did their French counterparts. This was also reflected in their concern for movement into segments of the industry which were likely to be high growth. The French tended to be more concerned with new products and the general need for improvement in products and services. When the analysis considered the four industries individually, similar differences were found.

The Calori *et al.* study illustrates the potential of the cognitive approach. The authors' findings indicate that there is a national cultural component which generates consistent differences between British and French managers, and which can be identified using cognitive-analytic tools. The cross-cultural differences found are attributed to factors at the individual or the organizational level, and sometimes both. For example, the British focus on short-term profits is seen to stem both from an individual concern with shareholders and from the institutional relations that firms maintain with banks. By uncovering the cognitive maps that managers employ in understanding their environment the researcher can begin to track those differences to their sources.

The finding that there were differences in the cognitive maps of managers across the four industries (automobile, brewing, publishing and banking) is hardly surprising. This finding supports the contention of Hofstede *et al.* (1990) that industrial and professional cultures may affect individual behaviour. More importantly, Calori *et al.* (1992) reported that within each industry there were cultural differences in the maps that the managers generated. Despite the common cognitive structures derived from their industrial context, managers from different cultures interpreted the environment in contrasting ways. This might be extended to other levels. If informants were asked about the structure and dynamics of more limited domains – for example in the areas of decision-making, leadership or supervision – the professional level might well emerge. The important point for any researcher, but especially for one engaged in cross-cultural efforts, is that these techniques reveal the underlying links between the elements in the frame of reference.

The study also points out some of the possible difficulties with cognitively based cross-cultural research. The collection of data, if it is not to be constrained by artificially constructed categories – an important point in cross-cultural work – requires substantial interaction with the subjects. The resulting constraint on the number of subjects who may be included in a study may limit generalization of the findings or, as in the case of the Calori *et al.* (1992) study, limit the comparisons that can be made. Balancing these constraints is the fact that sampling should be simplified. Unless some specialist knowledge is needed, the cognitive map of one employee, a priori, ought to be as representative as that of another. This is not to say, of course, that they will be equivalent, but rather that each will provide a construct that taps the shared organizational reality.

It might also be objected that attempting to understand cognitive processes across cultures is a project fraught with difficulties. As it is difficult enough to determine the thought processes of a manager from the same culture as oneself, attempting to penetrate through the screens imposed by cultural differences would make such an enterprise all but impossible. We argue that it is precisely because the purpose of the cognitive approach is to uncover what is normally hidden that it is appropriate for cross-cultural research. The dominant form of cross-cultural research involves measuring a behaviour (or value) in two or more cultural settings. Differences are emphasized to the exclusion of similarities, and explained by reference either to general societal values or to specific socio-economic arrangements. Both the behaviours deemed worthy of notice and the causes to which they are attributed are categories imposed by the researcher.

If researchers utilize tools borrowed from cognitive sciences and adapted to organizational research, subjects can be allowed to generate their own categories and to nominate elements which fit into those categories. Even more importantly, the subjects can specify the links between categories. This may be very important for understanding which elements are important in, for example, the formation of strategy. The British and French contexts studied by Calori *et al.* (1992), while culturally distinct, share a common North European heritage. Similar comparisons using more culturally distant countries might generate very different categories.

Once they are generated, the categories can be analysed using techniques such as cognitive mapping, frames of reference or repertory grids. Using a cognitive approach produces elements and structures which are derived from the experience of the subject rather than the researcher. This does not mean that the researcher does not impose any limitations on the research process. The choice of the area of organizational behaviour on which to focus will, of course, limit the responses offered. However, use of the proper tools casts the conceptual net more widely. The discovery of a fifth cultural dimension by Hofstede and Bond (1988) stemmed from their using a research tool based on Confucian rather than Western modes of thought. The result was a dimension which the authors admit could not have been found using Western models with a Western sample. Their approach, though still highly structured, allowed for input from those immersed in the culture. Cognitive approaches, properly used, would widen that scope even further.

One of the problems of cross-cultural research that is highlighted by the use of cognitive techniques is that of language. Most cognitive techniques require that the researcher interpret in some way the categories offered by the subject (Dutton *et al.* 1989). Laukkanen (1994), for example, describes a two-stage mapping technique which begins by eliciting key issues to serve as anchor concepts. These are then used to provoke comparable discussions with subjects about important concepts and causal linkages. A researcher without fluency in the local language and a thorough understanding of its use might easily introduce misinterpretations at either stage. Even widely used languages such as English and Spanish have distinctive local variants that might prohibit, for example, an American speaker of English from effectively using cognitively based research tools (as well as other types) in India. The use of colleagues from the target cultures to assist in this type of research, as called for by Adler (1983), is the most obvious solution to this type of problem.

To this point the discussion has centred on the advantages of using cognitive analysis techniques. However, one of the major critiques that we, and numerous others, have levelled at traditional cross-cultural research is that it is inherently atheoretical. Can using a cognitive approach alleviate this problem even slightly? The first step would be to generate a series of comparable mappings across a number of cultures. It would be best if these mappings were of a more global topic, such as decision-making, rather than of a more limited issue. This would allow self-definition of the area so that all factors relevant to the subject could be included. These mappings could be examined for similarities, as those collected by Calori *et al.* (1992) were. More importantly, they could be examined for underlying patterns, especially in the area of causal linkages. There is a danger here that both the maps and the concepts included may be too general, but this possibility should be alleviated by pre-testing in several contrasting cultures to find the correct balance between a wide scope of inquiry and sufficient focus to bring out specific factors.

Once factors or patterns of factors have been identified the causal links from national culture, perhaps through other levels of culture, can be proposed and data gathered to illuminate them. The aim here is to understand what is consistent in the cognitive structures and processes of managers in a culture and then to link this backwards to aspects of the culture (values, practices, structures) that explain the differences. It is important to avoid labelling whatever differences emerge as the culture itself. If one did, one would simply have invented a new means of doing descriptive work. The identification of the link between culture and cognitive framework is itself also insufficient. For the theory or the framework to have real value the link between cognition and behaviour must also be made. If managers in two cultures both give government regulators a high profile in their frames of reference, does this lead them to actions which seek to neutralize the regulators, to circumvent them, to comply with the regulations or to try to change them? Which of these categories are salient for the culture in question? The activation of cognitive states is an important topic for a comparative theory.

The question remains: how useful is a cognitive approach in understanding the dilemmas facing managers in an international context? A partial answer can be seen in our discussion of the work of Calori *et al.* (1992). However, a more complete answer obviously awaits research designed specifically to address some of the implications of the cognitive model. In the interim the utility of the model can be assessed by examining some important questions from the current field of cross-cultural organizational behaviour from the cognitive view. It is to these questions that we turn in the Chapter 5.

SELECTED READINGS

Calori, R., Johnson, G. and Sarnin, P. (1992) 'French and British top managers' understanding of the structure and dynamics of their industries: a cognitive analysis and comparison', *British Journal of Management* 3: 61–78.

Hofstede, G., Neuijen, B., Ohayv, D. D. and Sanders, G. (1990) 'Measuring organizational cultures: a qualitative and quantitative study across twenty cases', *Administrative Science Quarterly* 35: 286–316.

Langfield-Smith, K. (1992) 'Exploring the need for a shared cognitive map', *Journal of Management Studies* 29: 349–68.

Laukkanen, M. (1994) 'Comparative cause mapping of organizational cognitions', *Organization Science* 5: 322–43.

Schneider, S. C. and Angelmar, R. (1993) 'Cognition in organizational analysis: who's minding the store?', *Organization Studies* 14: 347–74.

Smith. P. B. (1992) 'Organizational behaviour and national cultures', *British Journal of Management* 3: 39–51.

Walsh, J. P., Henderson, C. M. and Deighton, J. A. (1988) 'Negotiated belief structures and decision performance: an empirical investigation', *Organizational Behavior and Human Decision Processes* 42: 194–216.

Weick, K. E. (1990) 'Introduction: cartographic myths in organizations', in A. S. Huff (ed.) *Mapping Strategic Thought*, Chichester: Wiley.

5 People and culture

INTRODUCTION

As we argued in Chapter 1, one of the key developments in global management over the past decade has been the wider net cast by international operations within the organization. At one time international business was mainly the concern of top-level managers, but now employees at virtually any level may find themselves dealing with foreign customers or working on a development team that includes organizational members from several cultural backgrounds. Thus a larger proportion of the firm's personnel face cross-cultural considerations as part of their daily activities. This new level of international contact involves a wider range of skills from a greater number of the organization's employees, who are faced with interpreting and responding to the actions and attitudes of individuals and organizations operating in contexts quite different from their own. The addition of the international aspect has complicated not only the functions of managers but also the training and management of employees to carry out these expanded activities.

The main preoccupation of traditional studies in comparative organizational behaviour has been the identification of differences, mainly at the level of individual behaviour. While this approach helps to alert managers to potential pitfalls with respect to other cultures, most studies do little to help alleviate the long-term problems inherent in cross-cultural interaction. The fact that problems and solutions apply to one behavioural and cultural nexus tells us little about how they may be applied generally. Suggestions about how to negotiate with a Russian counterpart are of limited assistance in negotiating with a potential customer from Argentina. Nor do they provide much help for working with the Russians in other types of interactions. This means that training based on the current comparative literature has to proceed on a piecemeal basis rather than introducing a general approach to handling all cross-cultural interactions. The limitations in generalizability stemming from the lack of a coherent theoretical framework have implications for managers and trainers, as well as scholars in the field.

We argued in Chapter 4 that moving beyond current approaches to comparative organizational behaviour requires studies that illustrate how managers and other employees adapt their cognitive frameworks, their sense-making abilities, to new contexts. In Chapter 3 we examined some macro issues, especially those that touched on corporate strategy, to show how different approaches to the strategy-formation process and its execution are based on cultural norms. In this chapter we wish to turn to more micro-level issues which impact directly on the individuals in the organization to illustrate how a cognitive approach can provide both a critique of past work and a guide to new directions.

We have chosen to examine three basic issues: human resource management (HRM), leadership and the transfer or working practices. The first and perhaps most significant of these is human resource management. In the late 1980s and throughout the 1990s there has been a major shift in this field away from a preoccupation with the systems and procedures of personnel management toward an approach which is more strategically oriented. To this end, it appears that both academics and practitioners have sought to redefine the scope of the human resource (HR) function. Whether this is just a new form of rhetoric (Legge 1989) or reflects actual changes in practice is still an issue of some debate. What is more germane to our purpose is the way in which these ideas have become central to international management, as evidenced by the journals, articles and books which have appeared under the international HR banner.

Another issue which has generated a great deal of interest among both practitioners and academics is the notion of leadership. The lively debate over the components of leadership (Kirkpatrick and Locke 1991) and its importance for organizational success (Howell *et al.* 1990) has carried over into the international arena, where the main focus has been the variation of leadership styles among cultures and their transferability across cultures (Hofstede 1980b). For geographically diverse organizations which adopt a global approach to managing their workforce this is a serious concern.

Finally, we will look at the transfer of working practices across societal boundaries. Work in this field has had a long and productive history in organization studies. Early studies conducted by the Tavistock Institute in London focused on the failures of managers to recognize the effects of contrasting social systems, which are often transferred across borders together with technologies (e.g. Trist *et al.* 1963; Rice 1958). More recently there has been an explosion of writing on Japanese work practices stemming from the quest to discover why Japanese companies were outperforming their international competitors (e.g Ouchi 1981; Peters and Waterman 1982). All three sets of issues have important implications for the successful utilization of personnel in international firms.

INTERNATIONAL HUMAN RESOURCE MANAGEMENT

The field of HRM emerged in the 1980s as a reaction against the more functional approach embodied in personnel management. The competitive challenges faced by American firms, and the clear differences between American and Japanese personnel practices led to a more integrated, strategically oriented system for managing employees. According to Guest, 'the apparent novelty of HRM lies in the claim that by making full use of its human resources a firm will gain competitive advantage' (Guest 1990: 378). However, within the general umbrella of HRM there has been considerable controversy over the definition of HRM, its content in practice and how it differs from personnel management.

The literature on the development of HRM tends to highlight the concept's American origins. It is often presented as yet another organizational tool – following scientific management, the divisionalized organization and motivational theory – which has emerged from the US to become incorporated into managerial practice and academic writing worldwide. Guest suggests that the original HRM concept was heavily based on values which 'represent, in modified form, persisting themes in the American dream' (Guest 1990: 390). In particular, he cites a belief in the potential for human growth, a desire to improve opportunities for people at work and the reinforcement of strong leadership. HRM could thus be seen as a wholly indigenous solution to an emerging set of problems which sought to restore America's competitive edge by realigning the system of employee management with the values of society. Ouchi (1981) and Peters and Waterman (1982) suggested somewhat the same prescription, though Ouchi's formula had the distinction of uniting Japanese practice with what were seen as American values. If the initial shift to HRM was tied to the underlying values of the US, it was also accompanied by a fundamental shift in management's view of its employees. The workforce, at least in some American organizations, was no longer viewed as a group of individuals who needed to be closely supervised and managed, but rather, as a collection of human resources to be valued as a distinctive source of competitive advantage (Beaumont 1992; Storey 1992).

One of the key differences between the personnel-management approach and HRM was the link between strategy and the utilization of employees. According to Devanna *et al.*, the 'critical management task is to align the formal structure and human resource systems so that they drive the strategic objectives of the organization' (Devanna *et al.* 1984: 37). This was an American interpretation of and reaction to the perceived strength of Japanese personnel practices. This resulted in an HR function that was 'directed at developing coherent, planned and monitored policies on all aspects of the organization which influence or structure employee behavior such that these generate behaviors which support the achievement of organizational strategies' (T. A. R. Clark and Mallory 1996: 8). The integration of HRM and strategy in international firms meant that the role of personnel who linked the organization to its foreign counterparts, especially expatriates serving abroad, received greater attention.

The currents which shape policy choices within HRM can also be understood as the interplay of stakeholders' concerns (which may be contradictory) with situational factors such as labour-market conditions and legal constraints (Beer *et al.* 1985). These policy choices affect longer-term consequences such as individual well-being, organizational effectiveness and societal benefits. The model is essentially circular as the long-term consequences feed back to impact on stakeholder interests, situational factors and new policy choices. While it would be stretching the point to call this model a cognitive map, it does indicate ways in which cultural concerns may impact on the HRM policies implemented by a firm. For example, the policies of a firm based in France might be influenced by the high value put on social welfare issues. If the firm operated a subsidiary in the United States, where issues such as job security have a lower profile, its overall HRM policy would still be constrained by the general policies of the head office.

While the strategic management and stakeholder models illustrate different approaches to international HRM, the first being more rooted in the strategy literature and the second having its origins in the human relations tradition, some common themes have been identified (Beaumont 1992):

1 An integrated HR strategy is critical to the achievement of organizational effectiveness. The integrated system involves both the various HR functions and the overall strategy of the firm.
2 Responsibility for HRM decisions should be devolved to line managers.
3 There should be an emphasis on the development of a strong corporate culture to ensure that behaviours are consistent with the values and philosophy of management.
4 The HRM system should focus on the individual in terms of appraisal, training and reward systems.

According to T. A. R. Clark and Mallory (1996), some writers have argued that this basically American conception of HRM should be applicable to other national contexts. For example, they point to Poole's editorial (1990) for the first issue of the *International Journal of Human Resource Management*, in which he proposed the Beer *et al.* (1985) model as a useful basis for cross-national comparative analysis. He suggests that for the international scholarly and business communities this is the most influential model and perhaps the most familiar approach. The premises of the model are broad enough to be widely applicable. Its regular appearance in masters of business administration (MBA) programmes means that large numbers of the business community would be familiar with it.

The implication that the framework for a universal model of HRM already exists and that it provides a basis for further work is subject to some of the same criticisms that we applied to the convergence hypothesis in Chapter 2. The generality of the model leaves a great deal unexplained. What is interesting and what may be of relevance to managers faced with a multinational workforce lies not so much in individual beliefs about the importance of specific factors such as minimum wage levels or equity provisions, but, rather, in the salience of those issues for the manager and the society as a whole.

In addressing the issue of universalism in HRM, T. A. R. Clark and Mallory (1996) have argued that for a theory or practice to be successfully transferred between cultures the cultural profiles of the two countries must be similar. Basing their analysis of cultural prerequisites on Hofstede's clusters, they propose that HRM in its standard American version would transfer most readily into the management repertoire of nations characterized by:

- low power distance, which indicates a willingness to delegate responsibility for HR and a willingness of individual employees to take responsibility for their own development;
- low uncertainty avoidance, a recognition that there are risks attached to this delegation;
- high individualism, with its emphasis on the individual;
- high masculinity, which includes the recognition that the way employees are managed makes a critical difference to their effectiveness.

This implies that the principles of HRM outlined above would transfer most readily to the cluster of Anglo countries (the United Kingdom, Australia, Canada, Ireland, New Zealand and, of course, the US) (T. A. R. Clark and Mallory 1996). Its applicability elsewhere would presumably depend both on the overall cultural distance between the US and the target country, and on the degree of separation on specific dimensions.

In a more limited attempt to formulate a universalist approach, Brewster (1993) has proposed a European model of HRM which explicitly recognizes the institutional differences in employee relations between Europe and the US. This distinction is not, of course, an entirely new proposition. As Pieper notes, 'the industrialized nations of the Western world have developed characteristic approaches to HRM which do show some similarities, but are different, often contradictory in many aspects. It seems that in practice a single universal HRM concept does not exist' (Pieper 1990: 11). Pieper goes on to suggest that the crucial discriminating dimension accounting for differences is the degree to which cultures are, in Hofstede's terms, collective or individualistic. This has several implications for the ways in which individuals expect to be managed and for their reaction to management practices.

Even if there is no universal understanding of what comprises HRM there may still be similarities in how HR is constructed and used in various cultures or cultural groups. T. A. R. Clark's (1996) collection sought to uncover what these understandings might be and to relate them to the relevant cultural and institutional contexts. In doing this, he was not only promoting a polycentric approach to comparative research but also looking at how sense-making processes worked in this particular but crucial area of management. He concludes that within the European nations discussed by his contributors there are three common elements of HRM which transcend national boundaries:

- a recognition of the importance of human resources as a source of competitive advantage;
- the delegation of responsibility for HR to firm and/or line managers;
- the integration and mutual reinforcement of HR strategies and overall strategy.

While these three basic principles may apply to several European nations, the societal environments that they contain still exhibit important cultural and institutional differences. Though there is evidence of convergence on some notions of HRM, relating work environments to HRM practices involves an understanding of the cultural and institutional contexts of different nations. For example, Sweden's strong collectivist culture inhibits the development of a more individualistic orientation towards matters of compensation and employer–management relationships, while the Dutch 'feminine' culture discourages Dutch employees from accepting 'hard' HRM practices (T. A. R. Clark and Pugh 1997). In France the presence of powerful owner-employers restricts the decentralization of HRM functions.

A more detailed examination of national differences in the HRM function can be seen in a comparison of the context in which British and German personnel managers operate (P. Lawrence 1991). The German personnel manager operates within a very highly defined set of legal constraints over specific work practices and under the structure of the federally mandated works councils. This means that German practitioners will take a much more formal approach to most HRM functions than their British counterparts and are less likely to be proactive in attempting to launch new policies or revise old ones. The legal element is so prevalent in German HRM that a law degree is a normal qualification for a personnel manager. The constraints on German managers also lead to the position having lower status and less professional recognition than in Britain.

If we make this comparison in cognitive terms – perhaps in terms of the cognitive maps that a typical German and British personnel manager would have – the potential difficulties of trying to move from one system to the other or trying to integrate the two within a single company can easily be seen. For the British manager, the personnel function is dominated by the relationships between employee groups – both local and national – the production units in the organization and specific work practices. A mapping of the British manager's cognitive space would show connections between specific issues, often particular work practices – in both his/her own firm and others in the industry – the personnel of the firm and the individuals, such as shop stewards, who represent them. For the German counterpart, the cognitive map is likely to include mandated bodies, such as the works council and various state and federal entities, as well as the body of rules that governs industrial relationships. Among other characteristics, the German map will be more static than that of the British personnel expert. The manager of an international firm with British and German units would need to take into account not only the existence of different laws and practices in the two countries, but also the contrasting ways in which the local managers understand their functions.

One of the functions of HRM most susceptible to cultural influence – and therefore most likely to arouse resentment when those influences are ignored – is performance appraisal. With the continuing expansion of global organizations and the concomitant demand for experienced international managers, the accurate assessment of managers and potential managers outside the home country becomes an important HRM function. Yet the understanding of what comprises good performance varies from culture to culture. In a study of performance appraisal in the United States and three Pacific Rim countries (Indonesia, Malaysia and Thailand) significant differences were found among the four countries (Vance *et al.* 1992). While the expected differences between the US and the three Asian countries were observed, for some measures there were also significant differences among Malaysia, Indonesia and Thailand. For example, on the issue of employee involvement in the appraisal process there were significant differences among all four countries, with Thai managers reporting the highest level of desired employee involvement and the Indonesians the lowest. The assumption that Asian or Pacific countries exhibit a standard pattern in contrast to Western societies is clearly unwarranted in this case.

There are also differences in the utilization of performance appraisals. A study by Zhu *et al.* (1996) compared the use of performance appraisals in Australia and China. In Australian organizations communication was an important function in the performance-appraisal process, especially in terms of allowing the subordinates to communicate their feelings about their accomplishments. In China assessments were more often used for determining pay levels and assisting in salary administration. In both countries development was one of the main purposes of assessment, but the Australians emphasized evaluation, identification and planning to a greater extent than the Chinese. Finally, the Chinese managers exhibited a stronger belief in the effectiveness of appraisals for improving performance and job satisfaction than did the Australians. Based on these results, Australian managers evaluating Chinese employees would find them less forthcoming than their countrymen and more apprehensive about the outcome of the process. Not only is the appraisal function different in the two countries, but its place in the work life of employees is quite distinct.

These contrasts in HRM functions across societies pose real problems for developing a consistent approach to managing human resources within a global corporation. There are a number of issues involved in the search for an effective international HRM policy. One of the important determinants of a firm's policy is the orientation of upper-level management. There are three general attitudes that the parent firm may adopt regarding international HRM: the *adaptive*, the *exportive* and the *integrative* (S. Taylor *et al.* 1996). Firms with an adaptive approach are less concerned with making practices consistent across societies and more concerned with fitting in with local practice. Organizations with an exportive attitude toward HRM stress rules and practices that can be applied to all settings. The integrative approach implies a consistent overall framework within which local standards are applied. Obviously, the parent's orientation will be influenced by the cultural expectations of the home country. One would expect, for example, that in a country where universalism is valued an exportive approach would be more common.

In addition to the parent's orientation there are a number of other factors which influence the international HRM policies a firm will adopt. The firm's international experience, including the degree of international involvement and its international strategy, has been shown to have an important impact (Adler and Ghadar 1990; Rosenzweig and Nohria 1994). External factors such as industrial sector and the cultural profile of the host country will also shape the formulation of HRM policy for a particular country (Schuler *et al.* 1993). These elements interact with the foreign subsidiaries' own HRM practices and the characteristics of various employee groups to determine local HRM strategy (S. Taylor *et al.* 1996).

In a study of US firms and their Mexican affiliates, Martinez and Ricks (1989) identified four factors that influenced the degree of parent influence over human resource decisions in subordinate units. The dependence of the affiliate on the parent and its overall importance to the organization were both related to greater influence by the parent over subsidiary HRM decisions. A greater percentage of expatriate managers in the subsidiary also led to greater parental influence, some of which flowed from the greater interest the parent evinced in decisions concerning the expatriates. It appears that a higher subsidiary profile within the firm was linked to more investment in human resources overall, and in expatriates in particular, leading to more headquarters intrusion in the management of those resources. Finally, a higher degree of subsidiary ownership by the parent was associated with higher levels of influence over personnel decisions. The design of the study did not allow for a comparison of parent and subsidiary personnel policies, so it is unclear whether greater parent influence led to closer congruence between parent and subsidiary policies, although the importance of expatriates and concern for their development would indicate that this is likely.

What does all this mean in practice? If we apply the cognitive model proposed in Chapter 4 to the results of the studies summarized in Table 5.1, it appears that there will be a number of influences on the way that HRM is practised and experienced in an international firm. The national culture surrounding a subsidiary will directly influence the expectations of local employees and the subsidiary's HRM professionals. Two corporate cultures, those of the parent and the subsidiary, will provide expectations for how the HRM function should be carried out. Depending on the strength of

Table 5.1 Representative studies of the effects of culture on human resource management

Issue	Study	Cultures examined	Findings
Definition of the human resource management function	P. Lawrence 1991	Germany and the United Kingdom	German HRM professionals are more formal, more bound by legal constraints
Performance appraisal	Vance *et al.* 1992	Indonesia, Malaysia, Thailand and the United States	Variance in understanding of good performance across all four countries
Performance appraisal	Zhu *et al.* 1996	Australia and China	Different emphases on the uses and importance of performance appraisals
Parent influence over subsidiary human resource decisions	Martinez and Ricks 1989	Mexico and the United States	More investment in personnel leads to more parental influence

the parent's corporate culture and its orientation towards its international approach to HRM, there may be shared cognitions among the corporate and subsidiary staff or there may be substantial areas of conflict. If the head of the subsidiary's HRM function shares a cognitive framework with that of his/her corporate counterpart, there is still likely to be some disjuncture between that set of beliefs and those of others in the subsidiary who have less exposure to corporate thinking. Any attempt to develop and promulgate an international HRM policy in support of global strategy should take into account these cognitive differences at both levels.

LEADERSHIP

While most available models of HRM have a distinctly American flavour, the literature on leadership is somewhat more eclectic. This stems in part from the wide variety of explanations that have been offered for the appearance and operation of leadership qualities, and the lack of consistent and convincing support for any of them. Researchers in the field have had a wide variety of models to apply to their own particular milieu. The widespread attention that leadership has received in the cross-cultural field also stems from the easily observable differences between leadership styles in different countries and the obvious connections with local culture. In one of his earliest articles, Hofstede (1980b) used leadership to illustrate national differences along his four dimensions of culture. His assertion that theories of organizational behaviour derived from the study of one country may not be applicable to other cultures has encouraged students of leadership to cast their nets widely.

Many of these studies derive from a very simple version of the naive comparative approach which involves focusing on a single country or a single culture with the comparison left to the reader. This type of work is, of course, inherently descriptive. Nonetheless it can provide useful insights into the roles and functions of leaders in a given society. An interesting example of this can be found in Khadra's (1990) analysis of the prophetic-caliphal model of leadership, in which he surveyed a sample of managers from the Middle East, asking to what degree they agreed with statements tapping the four underlying dimensions of the model: personalism, individualism, importance of the great man and lack of institution-alization. Support was found for all four dimensions, with the strongest support for the great-man disposition.

This study is interesting for several reasons. First, the link between managerial attitudes toward leadership and those of the society as a whole were explored through the use of confirmatory surveys. This is quite unusual in almost any form of cross-cultural research. Second, the author adopts a theory based on political roles in the region and applies it to a managerial context. The cross-over between the political and the managerial spheres is not just an interesting theoretical transfer; it also reflects the close relationship between the two roles in this region. Finally, the findings of the study – the emphasis on strong, even dominant types of leaders which Khadra believes limits managerial problem-solving – have direct implications for interactions with organizations in the region. What is left unanswered is the question of whether foreign managers would be seen in the same way. That is, is appropriate behaviour for local managers also seen as appropriate behaviour for expatriates?

One attempt to address this question can be found in the work of Morris and Pavett (1992). Their analysis of a plant located in the US and its virtually identical *maquiladora* counterpart in Mexico revealed differences in preferred styles of leadership even though the two plants showed almost identical productivity. They concluded that different approaches to leadership may be effective depending on cultural requirements. Since the Mexican and American samples were made up almost exclusively of native personnel (three American managers were included in the Mexican sample), there may also be support for the idea that a match between leadership style and culture is required. However, since there was no evidence of how successful the plants were relative to others in the industry, and since this was a single-firm study, generalizations must be limited.

Black and Porter (1991) addressed a related issue by studying the leadership behaviour of American managers in Hong Kong and comparing them with their colleagues working in the US and a sample of Hong Kong managers. They found that leadership behaviours were related to job performance only for the American managers working in the US. They concluded that the fit between leadership behaviour and effectiveness depends on the appropriateness of the behaviour to the culture. This can be interpreted in two ways. The type of behaviours required to achieve success may differ from culture to culture. This is one of the enduring themes in the comparative leadership literature. However, it might also be true that the definition of managerial success varies sufficiently for the type of behaviours which are effective in one culture to have negligible or even negative effects in another. One need only consider the types of leadership that would be appropriate in strongly individualistic and strongly collectivist societies to understand how leadership which is conducive to success in one leads to failure in another. Not only are the required tools different, but the target is altered as well.

A similar comparison of values among managers from the US, Hong Kong and China examined differences among a capitalist, a collectivist and a transitional society (Ralston *et al.* 1993). The study employed eight behavioural measures, four derived from Western theories (Machiavellianism, dogmatism, locus of control and intolerance of ambiguity) and four from Eastern theoretical bases (Confucian work dynamism, human-heartedness, integration and moral discipline). Systematic differences between the American and mainland Chinese managers were found for all the measures except moral discipline, but there was little difference between the mainland Chinese and Hong Kong managers. The authors conclude that there is little support for the idea that the growing importance of market forces around the world will cause a convergence of views among managers from different societies. They believe that existing value differences will persist for the foreseeable future. This would seem to imply that the values required of a leader would also be viewed differently across cultures.

Schmidt and Yeh (1992) pursue a similar theme in their comparison of leadership strategies among Australian, English, Taiwanese and Japanese managers. Using an instrument developed by Kipnis *et al.* (1980) to measure influence behaviour, they discovered differences in the ways that managers tried to influence their co-workers. For example, the use of reason as an influence strategy was given more weight by the Japanese and Taiwanese managers than the Australians, who, in turn, relied on it more than the English. Since convincing associates to act in accordance with one's wishes is one of the central functions of leadership, these results indicate another element of leadership that does appear to vary across cultures.

There have also been attempts to place the leadership issue in particular political, economic and organizational contexts. Schermerhorn and Nyaw (1990) argue that enterprises in China, through pervasive involvement in the lives of their employees, place greater demands on organizational leaders. Since the traditional work unit provides not only a place of employment, but also housing, education, medical and other facilities, the head of a large enterprise unit may have duties closer to those of the mayor of a small city than those of the CEO in a Western business. Many Chinese managers, especially at higher levels, have direct contact with the political system either through their own roles as managers or through their connections with political elements in the firm. The roles of public official and political actor are over and above the basic management of business and operations systems. Purves's (1991) account of managing in a Chinese firm provides substantive support for this view.

While there seems to be little doubt that national culture shapes which leadership qualities are seen as desirable, there are a number of other factors which may interact with cultural values and norms to influence the definition of a successful leader. One possible factor which has seen little investigation is the role of gender. Given the variation in women's roles around the world and the legal structures that have been adopted in some nations to promote gender equity, one would expect some interaction between gender and leadership. In one of the very few studies to tackle this problem, male and female managers from four countries, Norway, Sweden, Australia and the US, were surveyed about leadership effectiveness (Gibson 1995). There were significant differences between genders across the four countries, with females emphasizing the facilitation of interaction, while males paid more attention to goal-setting. The country effect was also significant for some elements of leadership, with Australia differentiated from the other three countries. However, there was no interaction effect for gender and country on leadership effectiveness. This would indicate that, at least for these four countries, culture does not directly influence a gender-based definition of leadership. This may be due in part to the fact that all four countries included in the study are industrialized and have taken steps to encourage women to participate in the workforce. Comparisons with societies in which women have more traditional roles might well provide different results.

The importance of industrialization to a number of organizational behaviours has long been a concern of cross-cultural research. Advocates of the convergence theory discussed in Chapter 2 argue that increasing industrialization will drive organizations increasingly to resemble each other across nations. Can the same be said about leadership? A study of Turkish managers found that their beliefs about leadership were closer to those of other developing countries than to those of more industrialized countries (Kozan 1993). Using the results of an earlier study (Haire *et al.* 1966), a cluster analysis was performed which linked Turkey with China, India, Argentina and Greece. The author argues that industrialization provides greater scope for cultural differences in leadership, while less industrialized societies with greater power differentials rely more heavily on autocratic leadership styles. This contention is supported by the data from this study, but the lack of differentiation among the less industrialized countries might equally stem from the failure of the original instrument, designed in an industrialized country, to include items that would tap variation among societies with lower levels of industrial development.

Current research into leadership has moved away from identifying specific qualities that a leader must have, to examine how different situations require different leadership behaviour. Rodrigues (1990) has argued that the situation in which leadership is displayed may be more important than culture in influencing leaders' behaviour. For example, when a task is structured it requires directive leadership, but when it is unstructured participative leadership is more appropriate. While Rodrigues allows culture some influence, it seems likely that he underestimates its potential effect. In his analysis, culture affects behaviour directly through the values of potential leaders and their followers, but culture may also affect the definition of the situation through the structure of organizations and the manner in which individuals understand the problems they face. For example, in a culture with an aversion to uncertainty there would be a strong tendency, first, to avoid any situation which seemed ambiguous and, second, to redefine any problematic occurrence to lessen the ambiguity. Situation might define the type of leadership required but culture would influence the definition of the situation. Any effort to disentangle the effects of situation and culture on leadership must take into account not only culture's direct but also its indirect effects.

As with a number of behaviours that we have examined in this volume, there is strong evidence that culture at the national level influences what type of leadership is perceived as useful or appropriate. In a world where organizations are spreading across more cultures and involving employees from more nationalities, there is greater pressure on managers to show leadership that will be valid beyond their domestic milieu. Much of the current literature on international leadership has attempted to identify, usually through surveys, the qualities – such as flexibility or self-evaluation – that define effective international leaders. However, the majority of this research has been done from the parent firm's point of view. International leaders are evaluated in terms of their worth to the parent rather than in terms of the view of other units in the organization (the Morris and Pavett (1992) study discussed above is an exception to this trend). This provides little guidance as to the leader's effectiveness in other cultural contexts or in dealing with those from foreign subsidiaries or partners.

One of the key elements of leadership is how leaders understand the situations in which they must perform. The literature that is available, both that which compares leadership across cultures and that which seeks to describe the international leader, focuses on general styles of interaction between leader and followers. While these studies (summarized in Table 5.2) may provide useful information, they may also mask important differences in leadership behaviour. Leaders from two different countries may both be directive but they may impart their guidance in quite different ways. What is missing is an analysis of the frameworks managers use to understand situations and act upon them. The work by Calori *et al.* (1992) cited in Chapter 4 shows that French and British managers identified the same elements in their cognitive maps but emphasized different factors and different links among them in their analysis of the environment. If leadership is situation-specific different cognitive frameworks should require different types of leadership.

Table 5.2 Representative studies of the effects of culture on leadership

Issue	Study	Cultures examined	Findings
Preferred leadership style	Morris and Pavett 1992	Mexico and the United States	Culture influences preferences in leadership style
Managerial values	Ralston *et al.* 1993	China, Hong Kong and the United States	Cultural roots are more important than economic systems to managerial values
Influence behaviour	Schmidt and Yeh 1992	Australia, Japan, the United Kingdom and Taiwan	Culture affects the types of influence strategies employed
The influence of culture and gender on leadership	Gibson 1995	Australia, Norway, Sweden and the United States	No interaction effect of gender and culture on leadership
Industrialization and leadership	Kozan 1993	Turkey and several other countries	Less industrialization leads to more autocratic leadership styles

TRANSFER OF WORKING PRACTICES

One of the dominant topics in recent international and comparative literature has been the importation of Japanese forms of organization and management into other cultures. This '*banzai* bandwagon' has stemmed in no small part from a quest to determine how Japanese companies were outperforming their international competitors (Turner 1986) and how Western companies could compete by adopting Japanese techniques. For some commentators, this was a genuine quest for the factors which lead to the long-term viability of the enterprise. For others, it may have been motivated by the search for a quick fix to resolve an uncomfortable loss of competitiveness. For yet others, the inquiry may have been a source of consulting revenue or a means of obtaining guru status (Huczynski 1993), with much the same outcome.

The introduction of new work practices, whatever their origin, brings changes to organizations. The most influential of the early studies in this area was carried out by researchers from the Tavistock Institute in London, who were concerned with the social changes brought about by alterations in British coal-mining techniques (Trist and Bamforth 1951). The introduction of new production technology reconfigured the interaction among miners, which disrupted the close coordination the new methods required. Since this socio-technical approach emphasized the interaction of technology with human relations, the implications for transfering to another culture techniques developed under assumptions of one culture were readily apparent. Researchers soon turned their attention to the exportation of work practices to other countries.

One of the earliest of these studies is Rice's (1958) investigation into the introduction of new weaving technology into a textile mill in Ahmedebad, India. When the new technology was introduced it failed to provide the expected productivity improvements in terms of quality or quantity, although relations between employees and supervisors were good and the workers' morale appeared to be high. When the new machinery was installed work roles were reallocated to conform with US and British practices. With twelve specialized roles for twenty-nine operatives, there was a large number of possible work relationships among the group. The clear-cut task structure that had existed in the former operation was replaced with a more complicated network of coordination. This led to confusion over the responsibilities of the operatives and the operational priorities that each should be following. When a new product was introduced which required alterations to the weaving operations the confusion was exacerbated. The need for specialization and individual responsibility, which fit well with the British and American cultures, was at odds with the Indian reliance on group cooperation and problem-solving. The fragmented tasks offered the workers little satisfaction and inhibited the exercise of their normal work relationships. There was little or no psychological reward to be gained under the new regime by accomplishing their duties.

There were two possible routes to solving this problem. The first, to retain the present system but to increase control through more direct supervision, would not only have increased the costs of the operation but also have incurred some resentment of tighter control. The second possibility was to facilitate the emergence of an internal group structure by making the workers collectively responsible for the operation and output of a group of machines. This option required workers to share the specialized jobs rather than assign them to individuals. When the second option was adopted it increased both the quantity and quality of the cloth produced. The experiment was so successful that it was repeated in other plants, with similar success. A follow-up study twenty years later (E. J. Miller 1975) found that the autonomous group methods were still in use by the original group although external changes had led to alterations in other parts of the plant.

It is tempting to conclude from this and similar studies that imported methods of work operations can be adapted to local cultural conditions, but there are other factors which may impede or even block a successful transfer. In the 1970s British Leyland (BL) decided to adopt the widely admired flexible-production system employed in Sweden by Volvo. This system was based on the allocation of tasks to teams rather than individual workers so that the drudgery associated with short-term repetitive tasks could be alleviated by group control over task assignment and ordering. The automobiles in progress remained at stations, where groups might work on them for two or three hours, instead of passing by individual workers in less than a minute as they do in the traditional short-cycle, assembly-line process. However, when the Swedish system was adapted to BL's plant it was designed so that machines rather than workers controlled the pace of production. While this may have been partially due to cost considerations (Wild 1975), it also reflected the high level of suspicion that existed between British labour and management at the time. Eventually the plant was retooled and operated as a conventional short-cycle time-assembly plant; the innovative design was largely abandoned. In its final configuration almost no traces of the Swedish system remained.

One could rationalize the failure of the BL initiative by comparing the Scandinavian preference for collective activities and responsibilities with the individualist stance of the British, but this would ignore important institutional factors. The discrepancies between British and Swedish culture may well have contributed to the failure, but it was the wider labour-market parameters that scuttled the project before it had a fair trial. It seems likely that the labour relations climate in Britain at the time meant that almost any innovation suggested by a British firm, no matter what its origin, would fail. The more important cultural difference resided in the two societies' attitudes towards union–management relations rather than in particular feelings about group versus individual responsibility. This was reflected in the organizational cultures of BL and Volvo, which were shaped and constrained by the national culture (Pontusson 1990). From the British workers' point of view any innovation, especially by a British firm, had first to be examined for nefarious intent. Swedish workers undoubtedly had their share of scepticism, but it was balanced by the possibility that the proposed change was a positive one. These attitudes were also reflected in management's general stance vis-à-vis its workers.

The interaction of culture and institutional context in the transfer of work practices is illustrated by the case of a joint venture by General Motors (GM) and Isuzu in the UK. The two companies installed Japanese work practices in an ailing plant, effected a significant cultural change and brought the operation back to profitability (Mabey and Mallory 1995). The change included retraining, job redefinition and a revised labour agreement. The success of this transformation, as against BL's failure, could be attributed to a number of factors: changes in the labour market introduced by the Thatcher government, a revitalization of the British automobile industry, more foreign investment or simply greater familiarity with production techniques from abroad. Since Japanese culture, like Swedish culture, has a strong collective component, the failure of the BL project and the success of the

GM–Isuzu joint venture cannot be laid solely at the door of that particular difference. Disparate cultural assumptions related to technology or work practices may be enough to undermine an attempted intercultural transfer, but other contextual factors, some of which will themselves be influenced by culture, will also intervene.

With the expansion of Japanese companies abroad, their working practices, which are strongly embedded in Japanese culture, have been exported to a large number of countries. In many instances the Japanese have preferred to build facilities from the ground up rather than buy existing operations. In part, this was to insure that plants were designed to their specific needs. Investing in greenfield sites also avoided the problems of changing structures and work practices in ongoing operations. One exception to this tendency is the New United Motor Manufacturing, Inc. (NUMMI) joint venture which Toyota and GM launched in California. This operation has received considerable attention because it is one of the few unionized operations in which a Japanese firm has a significant interest. The project took a GM plant which had been closed, redesigned it using Japanese production principles, and staffed it with Japanese managers and local employees, most of whom had worked in the former GM plant.

From a commercial and operational point of view the plant has been a success (Wilms *et al.* 1994). The American employees learned the Japanese work system to such an extent that Toyota was able to reduce the number of Japanese managers and trainers on the site significantly. However, friction remains over several of the practices that were introduced. One of the most contentious is the Japanese attempt to control absenteeism. Unlike American plants, NUMMI (and other Japanese plants) does not maintain a large roster of casual workers who fill in for absent colleagues. Absenteeism is treated severely in terms of both the individual worker and its impact on the team. The American workers see this as unnecessary pressure, the Japanese as a demonstration of loyalty to the firm. Problems with the ergonomic stresses imposed by the design of the production process and the pace of the work have also emerged (Berggren 1994).

The strains that have emerged at NUMMI and other Japanese plants in North America could be put down to basic cultural differences, that is, to the contrasts in certain cultural values or dimensions that occur at the societal level but are manifest in individual behaviour. There is evidence, however, that the difficulties in transferring work practices have more systemic origins. Many of the problems with lean production to which the American workforce objects are also items of contention in Japan (Berggren 1994). Younger Japanese workers are reluctant to accept the working conditions in local plants despite relatively high salaries and the prospect of job security. However, once they accept employment their position in the organization becomes an important part of their identity and they accept their obligations toward the firm. The Americans, in contrast, will use conditions as an excuse to exit the organization should other opportunities arise. Their whole understanding of the work situation is at odds with that of Japanese doing the same job. The cognitive framework in which they operate provides quite different interpretations of the social system surrounding the physical task.

The need to transfer techniques of operation and their associated working practices increases as firms move towards global integration. The studies summarized in Table 5.3 move from the export of technology in the 1950s to the integration of two manufacturing systems at NUMMI. With tighter integration of worldwide production, the usual tension between local adaptation and

Table 5.3 Representative studies of cross-cultural transfer of work practices

Issue	Study	Cultures examined	Findings
Adaptation to new work practices	Rice 1958	India and the United Kingdom	Work practices need to be adapted to new cultures
Transferability of work practices	Wild 1975	Sweden and the United Kingdom	In addition to culture, there are important social barriers to the importation of work practices
Requirements for successful transfer of work practices	Mabey and Mallory 1995	Japan and the United Kingdom	Cultural factors may interact with contextual factors
Sources of tension in work-practice transfer	Berggren 1994	Japan and the United States	Tensions remain even in successful cross-cultural transfers

economies of scale takes on a new and more immediate character. When international automobile firms try to design a 'world car', this implies manufacturing practices which are consistent at all their plants no matter where they are located. In some cultures the American or Japanese or German way of working will conflict with the expectations of local employees. Extensive training and the prospect of well-paying jobs may convince workers to conform to the system's requirements, but the tensions will remain not only at the operational level but also in the interaction between line workers and supervisors, who must enforce the regime even though they themselves may be local employees. The greater drive for worldwide uniformity will be constrained by the stresses imposed by confronting national cultures. Promoting a strong corporate culture, as Japanese firms do, can partially overcome these tensions, but apparently more by displacing them to the social level than by doing away with them entirely.

PEOPLE, INTERNATIONAL SYSTEMS AND COGNITION

In an effort to turn their firms into global operations managers have come to realize that they must find consistent international tools for the utilization of human resources just as they must for physical and financial resources. To assist them in their search they have access to two distinct bodies of literature. The first, the older literature, emphasizes the differences between cultures in the way that employees experience work and the social setting in which it is performed. This literature has amply demonstrated that important differences exist in expectations of leaders, in the means and outcomes of performance evaluation, and in the expectations that workers have of their involvement in the work process and its organization. At the moment, this literature of difference is being expanded to take into account more cultures and more managerial functions.

The second type of literature, which is of much more recent origin, focuses on the requirements for an international approach to managing people. For the most part, this research has aimed at uncovering the psychological traits or managerial skills needed to operate in cross-cultural settings. Whereas the literature of difference generally contrasts behaviour in two or three countries, the global literature searches for tools that are effective across all boundaries. In order to discover the necessary traits or skills, researchers have generally resorted to surveys, often of the practitioners themselves, usually at higher levels in the parent companies.

What has generally been lacking is any conjunction between the two approaches. The literature of difference usually concludes by exhorting managers to be attentive to problems caused by cultural factors, the implication being that once the problems, or at least the cultural differences at their source, have been identified their solution is obvious. From the global point of view, where a manager is faced with dozens of such contrasts, the solution is anything but obvious. An adaptation to fit policy to one culture may exacerbate problems with another, while ignoring specific differences in practice or orientation may lead to resentment and confusion.

The lack of connection between the two views can also be seen in the levels of the organization at which the analysis is placed. The difference approach habitually taps the behaviours and feelings of those immersed in the local culture, operational workers and local managers. Because the intent is to demonstrate cultural separation, those who are immersed in the culture are the logical subjects. The global view normally needs subjects who have just that, a global view. The result is that the level at which many of the stresses of cultural conflict are felt, the intermediate level between subsidiary and parent, is largely left out of the equation.

What is needed is a model which integrates the particular insights of the difference literature with the systemic demands of the global literature. The cognitive approach outlined in Chapter 4 presents a framework for moving from the level of culture to that of individual behaviour. It allows for culture, or multiple cultures, to act through structural and organizational characteristics at various levels. In the final chapter (Chapter 6) we will suggest some ways in which the cognitive approach can be employed to build on existing comparative research and inform its application to global management concerns.

SELECTED READINGS

Berggren, C. (1994) 'NUMMI vs. Uddevalla', *Sloan Management Review* 35(2): 37–49.

Black, J. S. and Porter, L. W. (1991) 'Managerial behaviors and job performance: a successful manager in Los Angeles may not succeed in Hong Kong', *Journal of International Business Studies* 22: 99–113.

Brewster, C. (1993) 'Developing a "European" model of human resource management', *International Journal of Human Resource Management* 4: 765–84.

Clark, T. A. R. and Mallory, G. R. (1996) 'The cultural relativity of human resource management: is there a universal model?', in T. A. R. Clark (ed.) *European Human Resource Management*, Oxford: Blackwell.

Gibson, C. B. (1995) 'An investigation of gender differences in leadership across four countries', *Journal of International Business Studies* 26: 255–79.

Pontusson, J. (1990) 'The politics of new technology and job redesign: a comparison of Volvo and British Leyland', *Economic and Industrial Democracy* 11: 311–16.

Rodrigues, C. A. (1990) 'The situation and national culture as contingencies for leadership behavior: two conceptual models', *Advances in International Comparative Management* 5: 51–68.

Taylor, S., Beechler, S. and Napier, N. (1996) 'Toward an integrative model of strategic international human resource management', *Academy of Management Review* 21: 959–85.

6 A cognitive approach to international management

THE FOUR- (OR FIVE-) DIMENSIONAL CAGE

The growth of interest in international business has been reflected in a large number of publications which try to bring some order to the comparative organizational behaviour field. Hickson and Pugh (1995) have recently published a treatment that attempts to pull together research on a regional basis, grouping together countries with similar cultures and highlighting their defining characteristics. While much of their information has been gleaned from studies in the naive comparative tradition, they utilize Hofstede's (1980a) dimensions to locate their regions in cultural space.

The degree to which Hickson and Pugh (1995) found Hofstede's approach to be sympathetic to their own can be seen by the fact that their efforts parallel three aspects of his work. First, Hofstede places great emphasis on the differences to be found in the cultural underpinnings of national societies. As he says in the introduction to *Culture's Consequences*, the Nazi invasion of the Netherlands in his youth had a profound effect on his career. The question of how two closely related societies could behave in such different ways motivated his interest in cross-cultural comparisons. The evidence presented by Hickson and Pugh, and indeed much of the work cited in this book, underlines the cultural diversity that attracted Hofstede's attention and demonstrates that it has important consequences at both the individual and organizational levels. The Hickson and Pugh book contains dozens of vignettes which highlight behavioural differences among managers. Hickson and Pugh's work, building on Hofstede's, demonstrates that cultural differences are real, measurable and important for the operation of international business.

Hickson and Pugh also support the existence and content of the cultural dimensions that have become the basis for Hofstede's approach. Not only do the dimensions provide a means of comparing multiple cultures, they also provide a baseline which allows other researchers to generate hypotheses and compare results. If it is true, as Redding (1994) claims, that Hofstede's work has become a partial paradigm for research in comparative organizational behaviour, it is the empirical foundation of the dimensions rather than the conceptual focus on values which provides the framework for future research. The cultural dimensions are intuitively appealing and have been successfully utilized in a number of works (Sondergaard 1994). Moreover, the ways in which different countries cluster on the dimensions seem to fit with other cultural markers. The Hickson and Pugh (1995) book concentrates on some of these groups and uses their location on Hofstede's dimensions to introduce each chapter.

A more subtle connection between the two works lies in the emphasis placed on the interaction of history and culture. When describing the characteristics that distinguish the Latin group of countries, Hickson and Pugh link the rule of the Roman Empire to a preference for more hierarchical modes of control found in the countries of southern Europe and their former colonies in Latin America. For them, culture is located in the values and beliefs handed down from generation to generation with roots that may stretch back to prehistory. While Hofstede writes more about the general significance of his cultural dimensions than about their impact on particular countries, the persistence of culture is an important theme in his work. More recent historical events are seen as playing themselves out within the constraints of culture rather than modifying the cultural substructure which shapes society.

Despite the importance of his work and the obvious influence it has had on the field there are a number of ways in which the looming presence of Hofstede's framework has limited the field of comparative organizational behaviour. Because his work is easily understandable and he has been at pains to make it accessible, Hofstede's approach has not only been adopted by researchers in the field but also become the standard framework to use when presenting comparative concepts to students and practitioners. One of the factors that makes it attractive is the ability to compare numerous countries on one or two dimensions rather than having to try to integrate a wide variety of binational comparisons. The availability of basic measures of culture – always one of the most difficult aspects of cross-cultural research – has provided a benchmark that relieves researchers of one of their more difficult and problematic tasks, assessing the national culture as a whole. One need not compile cultural profiles of Brazil and Sweden for a comparison; the numbers which provide them are already there, even though the data is now nearly thirty years old. In this way Hofstede's work has greatly facilitated the expansion of cross-cultural research; but in other ways the widespread influence of this approach has limited the growth of the field, especially in the area of theoretical development.

One of the major limitations of the Hofstede approach is that it is basically static. Despite his discussion of possible changes in culture (Hofstede 1980a: 342–71) Hofstede clearly regards values as relatively unchanging. The values that are fundamental to a culture are passed down from generation to generation and change only gradually. This reflects the anthropological view of culture, originally developed through the study of traditional societies, and which has been most influential in comparative studies. The more sociological view which has emerged in the last decade regards culture as a dynamic manifestation of contradictory social and economic currents (Alvesson 1993). Basic values in a society interact with changing economic and political conditions to produce altered expectations with regard to attitudes and behaviour. Even if we assume that the underlying values remain unchanged, events such as the introduction of a market economy in the countries of the former Soviet Union are bound to cause a shift in how those values manifest themselves. Such events may even, in time, change the values themselves.

There is no doubt that both the anthropological and the sociological views have utility when one is trying to understand human behaviour, but focusing only on the basic values of a society may mask important changes both in the importance of specific values and their articulation via current behaviour. For example, the value of equal treatment for all has shifted in many Western societies to include women as equals in areas from which they were formerly excluded. One can argue that the basic value has not been altered, but the behaviours to which it applies have changed dramatically. Regarding cultural values as given for a society makes it more difficult to analyse these changes or to develop a theory that includes explanations for these types of change.

The lack of a dynamic element in Hofstede's basic conceptualization of culture is parallelled by the absence of theoretical development within the framework itself. Of course, in this Hofstede is not much different from the rest of the comparative field. His earlier writings, specifically *Culture's Consequences* (1980a), contained references to various theoretical approaches, mainly drawn from psychology, which were more sophisticated than the majority of the work which had preceded them. But Hofstede's own work and that of his followers have moved away from any consistent theoretical attachment. In its orientation toward theory the dimensional approach has been static if not retrograde.

The static nature of Hofstede's vision stems not just from the basic concept of culture but from the set of research problems that this poses for researchers who embrace it. The greatest strength of Hofstede's work has always been the four basic dimensions of culture (now five) and the empirical justification that underlies them. While the constructs have been challenged (see Chapter 2), they have become the standard means of accessing cultural differences among nations. Since the general acceptance of his work, much of the research task in comparative organizational behaviour has been reduced to correlating various organizational functions (e.g. strategy formulation) or individual qualities (e.g. leadership) with Hofstede's dimensions or their equivalent. The crucial issue of describing the organizational and behavioural mechanisms that link the various levels of culture to organizational behaviour has gone largely unexamined.

Hofstede and his colleagues have addressed the linkage between culture at the societal level and individual behaviour as a methodological but not a theoretical issue (Hofstede 1985; Hofstede *et al.* 1990). Hofstede has been criticized for aggregating data collected at the individual level to compile characterizations of a whole society. To us, this seems less problematic than the next logical step, the application of societal characteristics to individual behaviours. If there is a generalized tendency within a society to hold certain values, then there are two difficulties in moving from that tendency to individual behaviour, the locus of behaviour which both managers and researchers are interested in understanding. The first problem, one which Hofstede himself discusses, is that within any grouping as large as a society there will be considerable variance in the degree to which individuals adhere to any set of values. It may even be that individuals in certain positions are more likely to reject specific values. For example, in societies where fatalism towards or acceptance of environmental constraints is seen as a positive value successful entrepreneurs are less likely to score high on those values. Similarly, in multicultural societies the degree of variance is likely to be higher than in societies dominated by a single culture. Generalizing from a single, uniform set of dimensional values to the behaviour of the individual across the desk is likely to be less than accurate.

Moving from culture at the societal level to individual behaviour is also complicated by the various ways in which culture may affect the individual. As indicated in Chapter 4, culture at the societal level may affect the individual directly, through organizational culture or through organizational cognition. Hofstede has argued that the organizational and societal levels of culture are relatively unconnected (Hofstede *et al.* 1990). This would apparently mean that the two levels act upon different behaviours, which seems to us an untenable position, or that the two will interact in some way even though they do not affect each other directly. We think it is more likely that societal culture affects organizational culture (and perhaps, in exceptional circumstances, vice versa) and that the two levels of culture may have contradictory effects on organizational behaviour. This consideration also makes it difficult to apply to individual or group behaviour any direct inference from characterizations of culture derived from the societal level.

All this is not to say that culture conceived of and measured at the societal level is not important. The field of comparative organizational behaviour would be rather barren if national culture did not matter. Nor are we trying to argue that Hofstede's work in relating national culture to behavioural tendencies is in some way incorrect. At a time when the comparative field was being called upon to deliver more insight into the problems of international management and was being castigated by its critics for being unable to do so, Hofstede's work provided a framework, both intellectual and empirical, which moved the field ahead and gave it more coherence than it had yet seen. What we are saying is that the solid foundation which Hofstede provided in the early 1980s has now evolved into a cage which constrains the development of a more subtle, more sophisticated and more theoretically based approach to understanding the effects of culture on individuals, groups and organizations. Developing a useful theory of comparative organizational behaviour requires that we move out of that cage.

ISSUES FOR A COGNITIVE THEORY

As we explained in Chapter 4, the cognitive approach to comparative organizational behaviour is built around the task of understanding the frameworks through which individuals interpret their world. These frameworks consist of categories to which phenomena can be assigned, the interconnections between categories and their links to behaviour. The model of comparative organizational behaviour that we have proposed includes two levels of culture, the national and the organizational, and two levels of cognitive framework, the individual and organizational. The main aim of the model is to evaluate the influence of national culture on individual behaviour and to specify other elements (e.g. organizational culture) that may mediate between the two.

There are two major groups of issues which must be addressed in developing a cognitive theory of comparative organizational behaviour. One set occurs at the level of the model itself. Throughout this book we have argued that one of the most serious deficits in the field is the lack of explicit linking mechanisms between culture and behaviour. One of the key tasks for the elaboration of a useful theoretical model – whether the one proposed here or another – will be to explain how national culture, which may act at different levels, affects the behaviour of individuals, groups and organizations. How, for example, is the individual's understanding of hierarchy affected by national culture and how does this influence his/her evaluation of a leader? What are the specific elements of culture that may cause a leader to be perceived as effective or feeble, constructive or disruptive? It is not enough simply to know how societies vary on power distance; we also need to know how individuals experience and react to varying degrees of social separation in organizations. Via an understanding of how culture affects specific organizational behaviours a more general model of cultural impact can be constructed.

For the model as a whole, one of the most important tasks is evaluating the strengths of the various paths illustrated in Figure 4.5 to ascertain whether national, organizational or some other level of culture is most important in determining organizational behaviour.

This will be a complicated task since the relative importance of different levels of culture will vary from nation to nation. In a country with a thick and coherent national culture one would expect organizational culture to act mainly as a conduit for the cognitive structures articulated at the societal level. The effects of foreign cultures, such as that of an MNC on the culture of its subsidiaries, would be influenced by the depth of culture that obtained in the local context. For a society with a thinner, more diverse national culture, organizational culture may serve as a means for promoting a more homogeneous cognitive framework among the subsidiary's members. Where more than one culture exists, in multicultural countries or in widely-dispersed firms, general effects on individuals may be difficult to ascertain.

The influence of national culture will also depend on the type of behaviour being examined. The impact on leadership behaviour, for example, may be quite different from that on group decision-making, even within the same country. One of the most useful outcomes of a programme of research into a cognitive model of comparative behaviour will be the sense of how important culture is overall. It has been an implicit assumption of much of the value-based literature that culture has an equivalent influence on behaviour across all societies. By means of a cognitive framework, the relative importance of culture, and its various levels, can be systematically evaluated for various behaviours across a wide range of societies.

To some degree, understanding cognitive processes across cultures remains a descriptive task even as we seek to integrate it into a theoretical framework. Research has shown that Japanese negotiators regard silence as a normal aspect of the negotiation process (Graham 1985). Negotiators from the United States and other Western countries are more likely to interpret silence as disapproval, or at least reluctance to participate. If we wish to build a more universal catalogue of behaviours and how they fit into the cognitive frameworks in various cultures we would need to know how silence is regarded in other cultures. What behaviours are stimulated by silence across the negotiating table (or in other social settings) and what is silence thought to signify? Of course, it is also possible that silence *per se* does not exist as a category in some cognitive frameworks. It might well be subsumed under other categories such as rest or peace. The specification of the behaviour under discussion may also be affected by cultural interpretations.

The second set of issues involves the application of the model to specific cross-cultural practices. One of the advantages of the cognitive model is that it allows for influences from more than one culture. The emerging international literature which seeks to identify effective approaches to managing multi-country organizations with employees from diverse cultural backgrounds has usually assumed that all foreign environments are equal or, more correctly, that they exhibit a set of universal contingencies which international managers must be prepared to face. While this is a useful approach in some ways, it often leads to rather bland recommendations on the aptitudes and roles required of international managers. The proposed cognitive model facilitates the inclusion of multiple cultures so that more refined research can lead to more specific directives. For example, one might investigate the comparative effect of disciplinary procedures across cultures by examining the influences of the national and organizational cultures on managers and line employees. This could be done with a sample of managers from one country and employees from another, a common situation found when expatriates are managing a local production facility.

In addition to testing the importance of the model's links, one may add additional factors to increase explanatory power or to clarify the action of sources of culture. One set of additional factors may lie in other levels of culture. Calori *et al.* (1992) and Hofstede *et al.* (1990) have argued that industries may possess distinctive cultures which affect organizational behaviour. Where closely integrated sectors such as the automobile industry maintain a worldwide presence certain specific cognitive structures may be shared across firms and so exert a general influence on organizational behaviour, especially at upper managerial levels, where interfirm contacts will be common. The emergence of strong regional groupings such as the European Union and the North American Free Trade Association (NAFTA) may, in time, also have their own identifiable effects.

APPROACHES AND ISSUES IN COGNITIVE RESEARCH

To illustrate how a cognitive approach, or rather a variety of cognitive approaches, can be used in studying comparative organizational behaviour we will examine four different methods, using each to suggest how it might be used to explore an important area in international management. The examples provided below are a small selection of the possibilities.

Cognitive maps and cross-cultural negotiation

One topic which is becoming more important for international management but is as yet insufficiently studied is cross-cultural negotiation. With the increasing volume of international business there is a growing necessity for business people from different societies to conclude arrangements through various sorts of bargaining. Successful negotiation, whether domestic or cross-cultural, has two basic requirements. The negotiator must first have a clear view of the goals he/she is trying to achieve and the way the various issues under discussion are interconnected. Since trade-offs lie at the heart of negotiation, participants have to know which concerns can be conceded to their counterparts, which must form part of any agreement and which can be left for the next encounter. Too often the negotiator loses sight of the original purpose of the negotiation as the process unfolds. Issues that seemed trivial in the initial evaluation may take on an artificial importance simply because the other side rejects or denigrates them. In the international context, because the process is often more complex and the issues less well defined, the possibility of overemphasizing trivial issues may be greater.

The second requirement is an appreciation of what one's counterpart wants from the negotiation. In structured, repetitive negotiations such as those between labour and management the desires of the other side are generally well known. In cross-cultural negotiations there may be much less clarity, partly because of different strategic agendas and partly because conventions of how much each side discloses vary among cultures. However, simply knowing what the other side wants is not sufficient. The internal trade-offs between issues and their operational links determine strategy and tactics at the table. Some of these connections may be made explicit but most will only emerge as the negotiation progresses. Experienced negotiators spend considerable time both before and during the negotiation process, assessing their opponents' position. Of course, in cross-cultural negotiations even straightforward attempts to clarify a position by one side or the other may be frustrated by communication difficulties or culturally induced differences in expectations.

Current work on international negotiation has emphasized the variations in the processes by which managers from different cultures attempt to achieve agreements. Researchers, usually employing a naive comparative approach, have investigated contrasts in process elements such as the type of argumentation used, the occurrence of negatives and refusals, and the relationship between initial offers and final settlements (Adler 1991; Graham 1985; Rajan and Graham 1991). What has been lacking is any investigation of issue-formation and the way that culture may affect both the salience of particular issues and the links among classes of issues. Of course, there is an interaction between negotiation process and the way that issues are accessed and treated during a negotiation, but the initial visualization of the issues shapes subsequent reconfigurations.

One possible approach to understanding the framing of issues for international negotiations is through using cognitive mapping techniques. In the study by Calori *et al.* (1992) cited in Chapter 2, cognitive maps for the strategic situation of European firms were solicited from upper-level managers. A similar approach could be used to elicit issues, their importance and their interconnections from negotiators involved in international bargaining. One of the advantages of the cognitive-mapping approach is that it provides not only lists of relevant issues but links among them as well (Huff 1990). This offers two advantages in studying international negotiations. First, it identifies the various pathways which may connect different issues. For example, in negotiations over the structure of a new joint venture one manager (or culture) may see the nationality of the top personnel as closely connected to issues of control, while another may see the two issues as relatively separate but connected to market knowledge. Second, a comparison between the maps of two parties in a negotiation could provide guidance for possible routes to compromise or mediation.

An examination of negotiators' cognitive maps collected from a single culture would allow researchers to assess whether there are consistencies in the way negotiators formulate their agendas. A single-culture sample would also reveal substantive similarities in the issues negotiators address and the degree of variation across the culture. One of the basic comparisons that might be made between cultures is the number of nodes that exist in a cognitive map, and the number and complexity of the connections among them. A more complex map would indicate greater scope for compromise but might also betoken greater difficulty in arriving at an acceptable package that would address enough of a party's needs. It might also indicate that a strategy of isolating groups of issues would help streamline the negotiation process. A simpler map would likely focus on a few issues which hold greater significance for that party. By building generic maps for a country or culture one could identify possible conflicts in styles of negotiation and design means for surmounting them. Collecting maps from different sectors within multicultural countries would yield an interesting test of how similar those cultures were.

The insight into negotiation generated by cognitive maps need not be limited to static comparisons. If a number of maps were collected from participants as the negotiation unfolded, the dynamics of the negotiation process could be matched to shifts, if any, in the underlying cognitive framework. This would be especially interesting if the negotiators were encountering a culture for the first time. No doubt cultures would differ in the degree to which maps shifted through the course of the negotiation and in the steps they took in attempting to match their cognitive framework to the negotiation process. This approach would require a more dynamic view of cognitive maps than has generally been the case in the organizational literature. Most mapping techniques attempt to tap the fundamental assumptions individuals make about the way their world, or a part of it, functions. It should be possible, however, to follow the changes that occur as the basic map is put into action and then must be modified, at least temporarily or superficially, to interpret the current situation. Once again the ability to make such accommodations is likely to be linked to national culture.

In addition to comparisons of maps and their effects on negotiations in different cultures, the same approach could be used to examine how experienced international negotiators differ from those with less exposure. Writers who study cross-cultural negotiation recommend that managers be flexible and creative in their approach to foreign counterparts. Do these types of attitudes show up in the maps of experienced, successful negotiators? Are there other common elements that can be identified? Are these elements similar across cultures for experienced negotiators or does the individual's home culture shape the way in which he/she is successful? Cognitive-mapping techniques cannot provide definitive answers to all these questions, but they can provide insights which have largely been lacking in current research.

Scripts and leadership across nations

Among researchers concerned with operating organizations across boundaries, especially those who adopt the internationalist view described in Chapter 2, the issue of leadership has been one of the most salient. In an era of globalization and dynamic change the role of the leader in providing a focus for the organization's efforts worldwide has become more and more important. The advent of simultaneous international satellite feeds and cheaply reproduced videos means that the head of a global corporation can speak quite directly to all his (rarely her) employees, even as the firm expands in size and geographic scope. The search for a set of traits and skills that will enable managers to act effectively on this worldwide stage as well as on the more mundane level of day-to-day communication have generated considerable interest.

Investigation into international leadership needs to incorporate two distinct perspectives. From headquarters, interest is focused on a set of criteria by which international managers can be selected and on skills which they can be taught. Both the criteria and the skills need to be universally applicable so that an international manager can operate anywhere the company does business. From the subsidiary perspective the emphasis is on possible conflicts between the leadership style of the parent's managers and that expected by the local workforce. Here the focus is much more on specific attitudes and actions, and the way they are perceived by local employees. Research from both perspectives has generally relied on measures of specific attitudes or behaviours to highlight differences in the concept of leadership in contrasting cultures or differences in effective and ineffective international leadership.

One difficulty with these approaches is that they provide a piecemeal analysis of a set of behaviours which are normally acted out and perceived as a complex whole. To find that an effective international manager should be flexible is useful as a general description, but it gives little guidance on how to approach a particular culture or task. It also ignores the fact that too much flexibility in some cultures will be interpreted as weakness or an inability to make decisions. What is needed is a more integrative approach that helps us understand the factors affecting the performance of leaders both from the perspective of overall utility and in the perceptions of specific cultures.

Within organizations, and sometimes for organizations as a whole, scripts outline accepted routines for reacting to common situations (Gioia *et al.* 1989). Scripts are akin to the sociological concept of roles in that they help to identify appropriate behaviours for an individual who is acting in a specific capacity. For example, the role of manager will include norms for acting as a disciplinarian when a subordinate makes an error or breaks company rules. Scripts tend to be more specific and directive than roles and may include multiple individuals, each of whom plays out his/her appropriate part of the script. As with roles, the effective performance of a script depends on all the actors, as well as any observers who are not participants, knowing what is expected. The lack of shared cognitive structures undermines a successful performance and may cause the script itself to be questioned. Scripts represent a cognitive approach to understanding organizational behaviour because they link the perception of a situation with structured responses to it.

Scripts are useful in understanding leadership in a comparative setting, because both the person acting as a leader (or attempting to do so) and those being led will have a script or a series of scripts which are appropriate for various settings. For example, the leader will have one script for facing a problem in the production process and another for dealing with important external clients. The scripts used by a particular manager are selected from those deemed appropriate by the organization, and are determined by the setting and the expectations of the actors involved. In a comparative setting all three of these elements are subject to change between cultures. The appropriateness of a script may vary from parent to subsidiary and among the subsidiaries themselves. The expectations of the actors, those who believe they will see a leader in action, certainly shift as cultural boundaries are crossed. The authoritative, paternal style common in Mexico will not be appropriate for Scandinavian subordinates, who may well not think of themselves as subordinates at all. Finally, the settings in which leadership behaviour may be expected differ from culture to culture. In some cultures leadership is largely confined to formal settings within the firm. In Japan leaders play important social roles outside the firm, in interactions with potential customers, important suppliers and government officials, as well as members of their own organization. By means of examining how scripts for leaders vary in availability and content across cultures, a more systematic taxonomy of appropriate and effective leadership can be generated.

Turning from the influences on scripts for particular cultures to scripts that may be used for international leadership raises another set of issues. Current literature identifies the ability to understand and integrate others' reactions as an important quality for international leaders. This introduces a new dynamic element into the concept of scripts. It implies, first, that effective international leaders would have a series of scripts available for presentation to the appropriate audience. This throws more attention on the cognitive aspect of scripts, the recognition of the context and the production of the appropriate behaviour. It also raises the issue of how general or specific such international scripts must be. If they are too general the performance may not elicit the desired response, either because it is not convincing or because it does not appear as the intended script. If the available scripts are too specific, then switching back and forth among them may make great demands on the leader, who, after all, has cultural constraints and commitments of his/her own. The degree to which more generalized scripts are useful will certainly be affected by the cultural context. Script-based analysis provides simultaneous access to the possibilities offered by diverse scripts and the limitations that may undermine their use.

The use of scripts for studying international and comparative leadership not only offers a new perspective but also suggests a shift in methodology that may prove useful. The majority of international leadership studies collect opinions about the characteristics, values or actions of effective leaders. While these results are useful, they omit the contingent aspect of leadership, in which these elements shape each other in the course of human interactions. Scripts offer a means by which subjects can be asked to evaluate or comment upon a richer version of leadership behaviours and to identify important elements or patterns. Actual performances of scripts can also be analysed to extract both the key interactions they contain and the sequence of behaviours the actors employ.

Making sense of strategic decisions in international business

The task of making strategic decisions in international business is becoming increasingly complicated and time-pressured as companies expand to new markets and the number of potential customers and competitors increase. The combination of a larger number of more diverse elements in the decision space and the need to react quickly to a dynamic environment means that managers tend to rely on heuristics and rules of thumb even for decisions which have major consequences. This approach works well when the factors which influence the decision are well known and their causal connections familiar. When circumstances are unusual, especially when they contradict modes of thinking that are embedded in organizational procedures and operations, additional efforts are needed to incorporate these new patterns. This is not simply a matter of recognizing new facts, but also of integrating them into new patterns of thought and action (Gioia and Thomas 1996).

Individuals are constantly making sense of the world as they perceive it by incorporating new information into their cognitive framework. Much of this behaviour involves the routine interpretation of events which map easily onto existing categories. The repetition of patterns confirms and elaborates them. Within groups or organizations important patterns may be manifested in symbols, either verbal (references to the 'Brown deal') or physical (a checklist for an operation). Sense-making, as it has been applied to managerial experience, has mainly focused on unusual events, those that do not readily match the available framework. In general this work has examined either the mechanisms by which new events or considerations have become incorporated into the cognitive frameworks of participants, or the consequences of failing to make sense of unprecedented or unrecognized situations. In some of the latter cases – most graphically Weick's (1993) analysis of the events detailed in MacLean's *Young Men and Fire* (1992) – the causes of sense-making failures are the object of analysis.

In comparative organizational behaviour sense-making can be used to analyse strategic decision-making behaviour in two basic ways. First, one can examine the operation of sense-making when a manager or group of managers makes a decision regarding an unfamiliar culture. This would probably be most obvious when the firm is entering a new market, although the purchase of technology from another country or hiring foreign personnel may also provide instances where significant sense-making will occur. There are a number of issues of interest here. Several of the works discussed in this book have relied on the idea of psychic or cultural distance as a determinant of success in adapting to a new situation (e.g. Kogut and Singh 1988). From this point of view, making sense of relevant factors from a distant culture would require more effort and cause more initial dislocation than making sense of those from a culture which has a similar value profile to the domestic society. However, considerable experience with multiple cultures may ameliorate these difficulties. Some of the mechanisms by which new cultural experiences are incorporated into cognitive frameworks can be isolated and examined by investigating how sensemaking occurs in the face of these new experiences. For example, individual managers or the organization itself may become proficient in making sense of new international cues through second-order learning (Argyris 1993). Then the object of sense-making transcends the under-standing of new cultures and their behaviours, and focuses on the process of sense-making itself.

The second possible use of sense-making in comparative research, and one which does not yet appear to have been implemented, would contrast sense-making behaviours across cultures. This could be done, for example, by examining the process of decision-making as an industry responds to the appearance of a new technology or the emergence of a new competitor. Given the rapidity with which such developments are communicated, organizations in different coun-tries should be responding to a roughly equivalent stimulus in a similar timeframe. Obviously it would be much easier to utilize sense-making techniques to examine group decisions, since at least some of the discussion will be public. This approach would also help to distinguish between the influence of individual predispositions and those which are more generally based in the local culture. The negotiation of a modified, shared, cognitive framework should highlight both the common elements in the individuals' frameworks and the strength of the underlying cultural base. It would not be impossible to study this process at an individual level, but more intrusive techniques, such as the use of protocols, would be needed. As with many cognitively based research tools, collaboration with a local colleague would help to ensure that the more egregious errors of interpretation were avoided.

There is, obviously, a certain complementarity between the two approaches. Some cultures have the reputation of being very slow to adapt to new ways of thinking. This tendency may be rooted in overall social conservatism or may simply be a preference for a view of the world that has proven effective in the past. Thus there may be cultural differences in how quickly and completely sense-making occurs, not only in general terms, but with specific regard to international issues. Just as members of a culture may interact differently with foreigners than they do with those from their own culture, sense-making may change depending on the source of the stimulus. Cultures could then be located (as shown in Figure 6.1) according to their propensity to utilize sense-making to revise cognitive frameworks due to domestic or foreign stimuli. It is, of course, possible that the two dimensions are closely related, that the majority of cultures lie in quadrants I and III, but the empirical issue is an important one for understanding the dynamics of adjusting cognitive frameworks.

This type of categorization would generate predictions about how sense-making would occur when decision-makers were faced with new or unusual circumstances. Both the sense-making and the strategic-decision-process literature (e.g. Mintzberg *et al.* 1976) show that the first response to a new situation is normally to seek an interpretation or solution from those at hand. Only when available alternatives have proven inadequate does the search for new information and new processes of assessing it begin. The fact that much of the information from a new culture will be difficult to

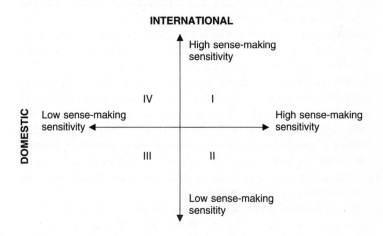

Figure 6.1 Sense-making sensitivity in international and domestic contexts

interpret could lead to longer search cycles and more resistant sense-making than if the new phenomena was from a familiar culture. Firms and cultures that reacted in this way would be located in quadrant II. On the other hand, the very familiarity of information categories within domestic or more familiar foreign cultures may inhibit more integrative types of sense-making since they would lead to well-known analytical routines and off-the-shelf solutions. These should be located in quadrant IV. The whole set of issues surrounding the contrast between domestic and international decisions – or, more realistically given the intrusiveness of international business, the contrast between strategic decisions with more or less international content – have yet to be investigated. Sense-making techniques provide an instructive conceptual frame-work and a useful methodology to explore them.

The language of international joint ventures

The final cognitive approach we wish to consider is one of the latest to emerge in the field. The study of language within work settings has developed a strong tradition, especially in Britain, but the majority of these studies have employed more formal modes of linguistic analysis, with an emphasis on grammar, semantics and the structural properties of sociolinguistics, for example conversation analysis (Drew and Heritage 1992). More recently, prompted in part by the postmodern emphasis on language and culture, organizational theorists have begun to examine how language shapes and reflects the underlying cognitive frameworks that govern organizational behaviour. Utilizing more qualitative analytical techniques, these approaches pay greater attention to the way discourse expresses the individual and collective reality of the speakers (e.g. Gilbert and Mulkay 1984). The use of language in organizations has been used to analyse the management of identity (Alvesson 1994), the exercise of control (Czarniawska-Joerges and Joerges 1990) and the conduct of performance evaluation (Gioia *et al.* 1989). In all of these, language is seen as an important component in the joint construction and maintenance of organizational reality.

The discourse-based approach to organizational language can be applied to comparative studies through the cognition–culture link advocated by Geertz (1983) and Bruner (1990): 'cultural products like language and other symbolic systems mediate thought and place their stamp on our representations of reality' (Bruner 1991: 3). The cognitive frameworks that are available to individuals and groups are shaped by the language in which their views may be expressed; these, in turn, are influenced by the culture of which the language is a part. In a comparative setting the different cultures provide templates for cognitive frameworks, which may reflect not only different values or beliefs but different forms of intelligence as well (Gardner 1983). Analysis of the language used by organizational members can help identify the cultural influences on their under-lying cognitive structures. This approach can be used to compare behaviours in separate cultures, but it is probably even more useful in investigating instances where representatives of two or more cultures must interact to create, at least temporarily, a set of shared cognitions. The international joint venture, which necessitates an ongoing mutual vision, provides a fertile setting for this type of inquiry.

Constructing a shared reality with sufficient coherence to allow for effective operation is one of the key problems facing the managers of international joint ventures, in which the partners often hold quite distinct understandings of the purpose, prospects and capabilities of the enterprise even after detailed agreements have been concluded. This leads to the partners and their representatives in the joint venture working at cross-purposes, or at least giving differential emphasis to competing goals. The lack of a shared understanding can also cause communication difficulties on a day-to-day basis if employees of the joint venture are drawn from more than one partner. While these difficulties may also arise in domestic joint ventures, language and cultural differences will complicate proceedings when the partners are drawn from more than one cultural setting.

In a study of an advertising agency, Alvesson (1994) analysed the role that discourse plays in maintaining professional identity for a group whose position is often tenuous. One of the tendencies he identified was the downgrading of clients' abilities and judgements by professionals. The dependency that the advertising workers felt and the necessity of asserting their own distinct competence led them to denigrate efforts by outsiders to claim ownership of ideas or to judge the results of the professionals' work. This occurred despite the need for clients and professionals to work together closely in order to carry out a successful campaign.

The same strains and responses are to be found in international joint ventures, and they are similarly likely to be reflected in the language used by those involved. Success in any joint venture requires that the partners – and the employees who represent them in the project, especially the managers – have a common understanding of the operation's agenda. Analyses of joint-venture failures often point to superficial agreement by the parties which is later belied by conflicting decisions and actions, and a lack of parental support for joint-venture activity. It appears that the initial labels applied by the partners may be the same or similar, but the understanding of what these mean, especially when they are put into action, are disparate.

This type of mutual misunderstanding might be studied in several ways. First, a comparison of the language used by each partner, especially the language pertaining to the particular strategic focus of the project, would indicate the degree of congruence that exists. Such analysis would need to focus not just on the labels that are used or their prevalence in discussions, but also on their relationship to other aspects of language use. For example, the elements of a common strategy for a joint venture might be embedded in a matrix of aggressive discourse, or phrased in a much more passive mode reflecting the partners' commitment to the venture or their overall strategic stance. Even though the same labels were used for the project's goals the linguistic context would substantially alter the implied meaning. The negotiations leading to agreement between the partners would be an important source of this type of discourse, but samples from each partner's internal discussions would provide language unmodified by concessions to another's expectations and thus might prove even more indicative of organizational language.

These types of comparisons could also serve as a basis for a more dynamic, longitudinal study of how the management of an international joint venture develops over time. With a baseline sample of organizational discourse from each partner, the evolution and modification of intra-joint-venture language could be modified over time. Since one of the major difficulties for the managers of joint ventures lies in the potential conflicts between the parents and the joint-venture vehicle, a shift away from the language of one parent towards that of the other would indicate that the cognitive framework is likewise shifting. If the shift is toward a form of discourse that is distinct from that of either parent, then the international joint venture will be moving toward the independent existence often required for project success. On the other hand, too great a distance or too much similarity to one partner or the other should signal potential difficulties. It is unlikely, at least in the first instance, that this type of analysis would be of direct use to the parties involved; however, it may prove a very useful tool for understanding the processes by which international joint ventures succeed and fail.

The study of organizational language may also help identify where conflicts arise in international joint ventures. A common type of international joint venture links a manufacturer in one country with a distributor in another. One partner brings technical expertise and perhaps product recognition to the project, while the other provides knowledge of the local market and access to retailers and customers. Such a partnership simultaneously introduces functional and cultural differences into the equation. Analysis of organizational language can help distinguish between these two sources of stress in the project and assist in mapping their interactions.

Scholars who work in English have both an advantage and a disadvantage in the use of language as an analytic tool. The advantage, of course, is that English has become the predominant language of cross-cultural communication. Since there are now more people in the world who speak English as an acquired rather than a native language, business people who do not share a common language are likely to use English as their medium of interchange. This greatly enlarges the scope of possible research sites and cross-cultural interactions which may be studied without help from translators. The disadvantage lies in the assumption that English is a standard language across these contexts. Linguists recognize numerous varieties of English with distinct grammars and patterns of discourse. In these situations a co-researcher familiar with local speech is as necessary as when working in a non-English setting.

BUILDING A COGNITIVE THEORY OF COMPARATIVE ORGANIZATIONAL BEHAVIOUR

The four combinations of method and topic discussed above illustrate both the scope of a cognitive approach to comparative organizational behaviour and the applicability of existing research techniques. The discussion also demonstrates how a cognitive perspective brings to light new issues and provides a new point of view for the analysis of persistent puzzles in the field. There are, of course, other techniques that may be imported from other disciplines which employ cognitive analysis, and numerous other issues in the international and comparative field to which they may be applied.

The next important step in the development of the cognitive approach is to accumulate a body of studies employing these and other cognitive research techniques. Such studies can serve as exemplars for other investigators wishing to enter the field, demonstrating how these methods can be applied and showing which approaches are most fruitful in which contexts. The brief bibliography at the end of this chapter lists some works which help illustrate both the techniques that may be employed in this type of research and the theoretical frameworks in which they have been placed. A growing portfolio of research will help to refine issues in comparative and international behaviour, and – since the cognitive approach focuses on the links between culture and behaviour – will bring to the surface questions which are not addressed by traditional approaches. Finally, and most important, cognitively based research will help to refine and expand the theoretical basis of the cognitive approach through the results produced.

The development of any theoretical stance requires that the structured relationships proposed in the theory be applied to actual phenomena. In the case of the proposed approach we are only at the threshold of theoretical development. The relationships outlined in Chapter 4 do not constitute a theory (Sutton and Staw 1995) but, rather, an attempt to show how culture may affect behaviour through the perceptions of individuals and groups, and how these perceptions may be shaped by the collective frameworks in which managers and employees of international business participate. It would be possible to construct a more formal and more detailed theory at this stage, but that would require the addition of variables which would diffuse the focus on what we regard as the key forces shaping behaviour in the international sphere. For the moment it is more important for those using a cognitive approach to construct competing or complementary explanations within the overall framework than it is to build a full-blown theory far in advance of any systematic evidence.

The conceptual and theoretical diversity that we hope will grow out of the cognitive approach should be augmented by cultural diversity. Since the basis of our argument lies in the influence of culture on cognitive activities, it follows that both the usefulness of the approach and the research functions it fulfils will depend, at least in part, on the cultural context in which it is employed and the culture of those utilizing it. We see this cultural ambiguity as a positive factor since it will subject the concepts and relationships to diverse interpretations from a variety of points of view. What better test of a theory of comparative behaviour than its ability to explain phenomena from numerous cultures in terms which all those cultures can understand?

SELECTED READINGS

Adler, N. J. (1991) *International Dimensions of Organizational Behavior*, 2nd edn, Belmont, CA: Wadsworth.

Alvesson, M. (1994) 'Talking in organizations: managing identity and impressions in an advertising agency', *Organization Studies* 15: 535–63. (The author uses organizational discourse to examine how employees of a Swedish advertising agency manage their problematic relationships with clients.)

Eden, C., Ackerman, F. and Cropper, S. (1992) 'The analysis of cause maps', *Journal of Management Studies* 29: 309–24. (A brief discussion of how cognitive maps may be analysed along with some of the limits of their interpretation.)

Fant, L. (1995) 'Negotiation discourse and interaction in a cross-cultural perspective: the case of Sweden and Spain', in K. Ehlich and J. Wagner (eds) *The Discourse of Business Negotiation*, Berlin: Mouton de Gruyter. (Illustrates the use of linguistic analysis to understand cultural differences in negotiation styles and outcomes.)

Gilbert, G. N. and Mulkay, M. (1984) *Opening Pandora's Box: A Sociological Analysis of Scientists' Discourse*, Cambridge: Cambridge University Press. (An investigation of a paradigm shift in the natural sciences analysed through the discourse of the scientists involved.)

Gioia, D. A. (1992) 'Pinto fires and personal ethics: a script analysis of missed opportunities', *Journal of Business Ethics* 11: 379–89. (Script analysis is used to analyse the author's role in a series of decisions relating to automobile safety.)

Gioia, D. A. and Poole, P. P. (1984) 'Scripts in organizational behavior', *Academy of Management Review* 9: 449–59. (An early discussion of the idea of scripts as cognitively-based guides to behaviour.)

Graham, J. L. (1985) 'The influence of culture on the process of business negotiations: an exploratory study', *Journal of International Business Studies* 16: 81–96. (An early and concise example of how negotiation styles vary among cultures.)

Huff, A. S. (1990) 'Mapping strategic thought' in A. S. Huff (ed.) *Mapping Strategic Thought*, Chicester: Wiley. (A very useful summary of different techniques of cognitive mapping.)

Weick, K. E. (1993) 'The collapse of sensemaking in organizations: the Mann Gulch disaster', *Administrative Science Quarterly* 38: 628–52. (An intriguing and affecting analysis of the worst disaster ever to strike the US Forest Service's smokejumpers.)

—— (1995) *Sensemaking in Organizations*, Thousand Oaks, CA: Sage. (A thorough treatment of the concept and process of sense-making and its implications for understanding organizations.)

References

Adler, N. J. (1983) 'Cross-cultural management research: the ostrich and the trend', *Academy of Management Review* 8: 226–32.

—— (1984) 'Understanding the ways of understanding: cross-cultural management methodology reviewed', *Advances in International Comparative Management* 1: 31–67.

—— (1991) *International Dimensions of Organizational Behavior*, 2nd edn, Belmont, CA: Wadsworth.

Adler, N. J. and Ghadar, F. (1990) 'Strategic human resource management: a global perspective', in R. Pieper (ed.) *Human Resource Management: An International Comparison*, Berlin: de Gruyter.

Adler, N. J. and Graham, J. L. (1989) 'Cross-cultural interaction: the international comparison fallacy?', *Journal of International Business Studies* 20: 515–37.

Aiken, M. and Bacharach, S. B. (1979) 'Culture and organizational structure and process: a comparative study of local government administrative bureaucracies in the Walloon and Flemish regions of Belgium', in C. J. Lammers and D. J. Hickson (eds) *Organizations Alike and Unlike*, London: Routledge & Kegan Paul.

Al-Aiban, K. M. and Pearce, J. L. (1993) 'The influence of values on management practices: a test in Saudi Arabia and the United States', *International Studies of Management and Organization* 23: 35–52.

Aldrich, H. E. (1972) 'Technology and organizational structure: a reexamination of the findings of the Aston group', *Administrative Science Quarterly* 17: 26–43.

Ali, A. J. (1989) 'Decision style and work satisfaction of Arab Gulf executives: a cross-national study', *International Studies of Management and Organization* 19(2): 22–37.

—— (1993) 'Decision-making style, individualism and attitudes toward risk of Arab executives', *International Studies of Management and Organization* 23(3): 53–73.

Allen, T. J. and Hauptman, O. (1990) 'The substitution of communication technologies for organizational structure in research and development', in

J. Fulk and C. W. Steinfield (eds) *Organizations and Communication Technology*, Newbury Park, CA: Sage.

Alvesson, M. (1993) *Cultural Perspectives on Organizations*, Cambridge: Cambridge University Press.

—— (1994) 'Talking in organizations: managing identity and impressions in an advertising agency', *Organization Studies* 15: 535–63.

Argyris, C. (1993) *On Organizational Learning*: Cambridge, MA: Blackwell.

Axelsson, R., Cray, D., Mallory, G. R. and Wilson, D. C. (1991) 'Decision style in British and Swedish organizations: a comparative examination of strategic decision making', *British Journal of Management* 2: 67–79.

Baird, I. S., Lyles, M. A. and Wharton, R. (1990) 'Attitudinal differences between American and Chinese managers regarding joint venture management', *Management International Review* 30: 53–68, special issue.

Barkema, H. G., Bell, J. H. and Pennings, J. M. (1996) 'Foreign entry, cultural barriers, and learning', *Strategic Management Journal* 17: 151–66.

Barrett, C. V. and Bass, B. M. (1976) 'Cross-cultural issues in industrial and organizational psychology', in M. D. Dunnette (ed.) *Handbook of Industrial and Organizational Psychology*, Chicago, IL: Rand McNally.

Bartlett, C. A. and Ghoshal, S. (1987) 'Managing across borders: new organizational responses', *Sloan Management Review* 29(1): 43–53.

—— (1989) 'Organizing for worldwide effectiveness: the transnational solution', *California Management Review* 31(1): 54–74.

Beaumont, P. B. (1992) 'The U.S. human resource literature: a review', in G. Salaman *et al.* (eds) *Human Resource Strategies*, London: Sage.

Beck, B. E. F. and Moore, L. F. (1985) 'Linking the host culture to organizational variables', in P. J. Frost *et al.* (eds) *Organizational Culture*, Beverly Hills, CA: Sage.

Beer, M., Spector, B., Laurence, P. R., Mills, D. Q. and Walton, R. E. (1985) *Human Resource Management: A General Manager's Perspective*, New York: Free Press.

Berggren, C. (1994) 'NUMMI vs. Uddevalla', *Sloan Management Review* 35(2): 37–49.

Black, J. S. and Porter, L. W. (1991) 'Managerial behaviors and job performance: a successful manager in Los Angeles may not succeed in Hong Kong', *Journal of International Business Studies* 22: 99–113.

Blankenburg, E. (1983) 'Review article', *Organization Studies* 4: 387–93.

Blau, P. M. and Schoenherr, R. A. (1971) *The Structure of Organizations*, New York: Basic Books.

Bougon, M., Weick, K. and Binkhorst, D. (1977) 'Cognition in organizations: an analysis of the Utrecht Jazz Orchestra', *Administrative Science Quarterly* 22: 606–39.

Boyacigiller, N. A. and Adler, N. J. (1991) 'The parochial dinosaur: organizational science in a global context', *Academy of Management Review* 16: 262–90.

Brewster, C. (1993) 'Developing a "European" model of human resource management', *International Journal of Human Resource Management* 4: 765–84.

Brown, L. T., Rugman, A. M. and Verbeke, A. (1989) 'Japanese joint ventures with Western multinationals: synthesizing the economic and cultural explanations for failure', *Asia Pacific Journal of Management* 6: 225–42.

Bruner, J. (1990) *Acts of Meaning*, Cambridge, MA: Harvard University Press.

—— (1991) 'The narrative construction of reality', *Critical Inquiry* 18: 1–21.

Buckley, P. J. and Casson, M. (1988) 'A theory of cooperation in international business', in F. J. Contractor and P. Lorange (eds) *Cooperative Strategies in International Business*, New York: Lexington Books.

Calori, R., Johnson, G. and Sarnin, P. (1992) 'French and British top managers' understanding of the structure and dynamics of their industries: a cognitive analysis and comparison', *British Journal of Management* 3: 61–78.

Calori, R., Lubatkin, M. and Very, P. (1994) 'Control mechanisms in cross-border acquisitions: an international comparison', *Organization Studies* 15: 361–79.

Campbell, D. T. and Stanley, J. C. (1966) *Experimental and Quasi-Experimental Designs for Research*, Chicago, IL: Rand-McNally.

Chandler, A. D. (1962) *Strategy and Structure: Chapters in the History of American Enterprise*, Cambridge, MA: MIT Press.

Chanlat, A. and Bedard, R. (1991) 'Managing in the Quebec style: originality and vulnerability', *International Studies of Management and Organization* 21: 10–37.

Channon, D. (1973) *The Strategy and Structure of British Enterprise*, London: Macmillan.

Chatterjee, S., Lubatkin, M. H., Schweiger, D. M. and Weber, Y. (1992) 'Cultural differences and shareholder value in related mergers: linking equity and human capital', *Strategic Management Journal* 13: 319–34.

Child, J. (1972) 'Organizational structures, environment and performance: the role of strategic choice', *Sociology* 6: 1–22.

—— (1981) 'Culture, contingency and capitalism in the cross-national study of organizations', *Research in Organizational Behavior* 3: 303–56.

Child, J. and Kieser, A. (1981) 'Organizations and managerial roles in British and West German companies: an examination of the culture-free thesis', in D. J. Hickson and C. J. McMillan (eds) *Organization and Nation: The Aston Programme IV*, Farnborough: Gower.

Clark, P. and Mueller, F. (1996) 'Organization and nations: from universalism to institutionalism?', *British Journal of Management* 7: 125–39.

Clark, T. A. R. (ed.) (1996) *European Human Resource Management*, Oxford: Blackwell.

Clark, T. A. R. and Mallory, G. R. (1995) 'The impact of strategic choice on the internationalization of the firm', in J. Clegg, G. Chryssochoidis and C. Millar (eds) *Internationalization Strategies*, London: Macmillan.
—— (1996) 'The cultural relativity of human resource management: is there a universal model?', in T. A. R. Clark (ed.) *European Human Resource Management*, Oxford: Blackwell.
Clark, T. A. R. and Pugh, D. (1997) 'Convergence and divergence in European HRM: an exploratory polycentric study', paper presented at the European Academy of Management Conference, Dublin, June.
Contractor, F. J. (1990) 'Ownership patterns of U.S. Joint Ventures abroad and the liberalization of foreign government regulations in the 1980s: evidence from the benchmark surveys', *Journal of International Business Studies* 21: 55–73.
Cray, D. (1994) 'Decision support for strategic decisions: specificity, generalization and timing', paper presented at the XIth International Conference on Multiple Criteria Decision Making, Coimbra, Portugal.
Cray, D. and Haines, G. H., Jr (1996) 'The relationship between environmental complexity and information processing structure and its effect on performance: the case of Canadian pension fund managers', *Journal of Information Technology Management* 6: 1–11.
Cullen, J. B., Johnson, J. L. and Sakano, T. (1995) 'Japanese and local partner commitment to IJVs: psychological consequences of outcomes and investments in the IJV relationship', *Journal of International Business Studies* 26: 91–115.
Czarniawska-Joerges, B. and Joerges, B. (1990) 'Linguistic artifacts at the service of organizational control', in P. Gagliardi (ed.) *Symbols and Artifacts: Views of the Corporate Landscape*, Berlin: de Gruyter.
Datta, D. K. (1991) 'Organizational fit and acquisition performance: effects of post-acquisition integration', *Strategic Management Journal* 12: 281–97.
Deal, T. E. and Kennedy, A. A. (1982) *Corporate Cultures: The Rites and Rituals of Corporate Life*, Reading, MA: Addison-Wesley.
Devanna, M. A., Fombrun, C. J. and Tichy, N. M. (1984) 'A framework for strategic human resource management', in C. J. Fombrun, N. M. Tichy, and M. A. Devanna (eds) *Strategic Human Resource Management*, New York: Wiley.
Donaldson, L. (1975) 'The Aston findings on centralization: further discussion', *Administrative Science Quarterly* 20: 453–56.
—— (1985) *In Defence of Organization Theory: A Reply to the Critics*, Cambridge: Cambridge University Press.
—— (1986) 'Size and bureaucracy in East and West: a preliminary meta-analysis', in S. R. Clegg, D. C. Dunphy and S. G. Redding, (eds) *The Enterprise and Management in East Asia*, Hong Kong: Centre of Asian Studies, University of Hong Kong.
Dorfman, P. W. and Howell, J. P. (1988) 'Dimensions of national culture and effective leadership patterns: Hofstede revisited', *Advances in International Comparative Management* 3: 127–50.

Douglas, S. P. and Wind, Y. (1987) 'The myth of globalization', *Columbia Journal of World Business* 22(4): 19–29.

Drenth, P. J. D. , Koopman, P. L., Rus, V., Odar, M., Heller, F. and Brown, A. (1979) 'Participative decision making: a comparative study', *Industrial Relations* 18: 295–309.

Drew, P and Heritage, J. (eds) (1992) *Talk at Work: Interaction in Institutional Settings*, Cambridge: Cambridge University Press.

Dubin, R. (1970) 'Management in Britain: impressions of a visiting professor', *Journal of Management Studies* 7: 183–98.

Dubinsky, A. J., Jolson, M. A., Kotabe, M. and Lim, C. U. (1991) 'A cross-national investigation of industrial salespeople's ethical perceptions', *Journal of International Business Studies* 22: 651–70.

Dunning, J. H. (1992) *Multinational Enterprises and the Global Economy*, Wokingham: Addison-Wesley.

Dunphy, D. C. (1986) 'An historical review of the literature on the Japanese enterprise and its management', in S. R. Clegg, D. C. Dunphy and S. G. Redding (eds) *The Enterprise and Management in East Asia*, Hong Kong: Centre of Asian Studies, University of Hong Kong.

Dutton, J. E., Walton, E. J., and Abrahmson, E. (1989) 'Important dimensions of strategic issues: separating the wheat from the chaff', *Journal of Management Studies* 26: 379–96.

Dyas, G. P. and Thanheiser, H. T. (1976) *The Emerging European Enterprise*, London: Macmillan.

Earley, P. C. and Singh, H. (1995) 'International and intercultural management research: what's next?', *Academy of Management Journal* 38: 327–40.

Eden, C. (1992) 'On the nature of cognitive maps', *Journal of Management Studies* 29: 261–5.

Eden, C., Ackerman, F. and Cropper, S. (1992) 'The analysis of cause maps', *Journal of Management Studies* 29: 309–24.

England, G. W. (1975) *The Manager and His Values*, Cambridge, MA: Ballinger.

Erramilli, M. K. (1996) 'Nationality and subsidiary ownership patterns in multinational corporations', *Journal of International Business Studies* 27: 225–48.

Fant, L. (1995) 'Negotiation discourse and interaction in a cross-cultural perspective: the case of Sweden and Spain', in K. Ehlich and J. Wagner (eds) *The Discourse of Business Negotiation*, Berlin: de Gruyter.

Fayol, H. (1949) *General and Industrial Management*, London: Pitman.

Fiol, C. M. and Huff, A. S. (1992) 'Maps for managers: where are we? Where do we go from here?', *Journal of Management Studies* 29: 267–85.

Fletcher, K. E. and Huff, A. S. (1990) 'Argument mapping', in A. S. Huff (ed.) *Mapping Strategic Thought*, Chicester: Wiley.

Gagliardi, P. (1986) 'The creation and change of organizational cultures: a conceptual framework', *Organization Studies* 7: 117–34.

Galbraith, J. R. and Nathanson, D. A. (1979) 'The role of organizational structure and process in strategy implementation', in D. E. Schendel and

C. W. Hofer (eds) *Strategic Management: A New View of Business Policy and Planning*, Boston, MA: Little Brown.

Gallie, D. (1978) *In Search of the New Working Class*, Cambridge: Cambridge University Press.

Ganitsky, J. and Watzke, G. E. (1990) 'Implications of different time perspectives for human resource management in international joint ventures', *Management International Review* 30: 37–51, special issue.

Gardner, H. (1983) *Frames of Mind: The Theory of Multiple Intelligences*, New York: Basic Books.

—— (1985) *The Mind's New Science: A History of the Cognitive Revolution*, New York: Basic Books.

Geertz, C. (1983) *Local Knowledge: Further Essays in Interpreting Anthropology*, New York: Basic Books.

Ghertman, M. (1988) 'Foreign subsidiary and parents' roles during strategic investment and divestment decisions', *Journal of International Business Studies* 19: 47–67.

Ghoshal, S. (1987) 'Global strategy: an organizing framework', *Strategic Management Journal* 8: 425–440.

Gibson, C. B. (1995) 'An investigation of gender differences in leadership across four countries', *Journal of International Business Studies* 26: 255–79.

Gilbert, G. N. and Mulkay, M. (1984) *Opening Pandora's Box: A Sociological Analysis of Scientists' Discourse*, Cambridge: Cambridge University Press.

Gioia, D. A. (1986) 'Symbols, scripts and sensemaking: creating meaning in the organizational experience', in H. P. Sims, Jr, and D. A. Gioia (eds) *The Thinking Organization*, San Francisco, CA: Jossey-Bass.

—— (1992) 'Pinto fires and personal ethics: a script analysis of missed opportunities', *Journal of Business Ethics* 11: 379–89.

Gioia, D. A., Donnellon, A. and Sims, H. P., Jr (1989) 'Communication and cognition in appraisal: a tale of two paradigms', *Organization Studies* 10: 503–29.

Gioia, D. A. and Poole, P. P. (1984) 'Scripts in organizational behavior', *Academy of Management Review* 9: 449–59.

Gioia, D. A. and Thomas, J. B. (1996) 'Identity, image and issue interpretation: sensemaking during strategic change in academia', *Administrative Science Quarterly* 41: 370–403.

Glick, W. H. (1985) 'Conceptualizing and measuring organizational and psychological climate: pitfalls in multilevel research', *Academy of Management Review* 10: 601–16.

Godkin, L, Braye, C. E. and Caunch, C. L. (1989) 'U.S.-based cross-cultural research in the eighties', *Journal of Business and Economic Perspectives* 15: 37–45.

Goodstein, L. D. (1981) 'American business values and cultural imperialism', *Organizational Dynamics* 10(1): 49–54.

Graham, J. L. (1985) 'The influence of culture on the process of business negotiations: an exploratory study', *Journal of International Business Studies* 16: 81–96.

Grant, R. M. (1991) 'The resource-based theory of competitive advantage: implications for strategy formulation', *California Management Review* 33(3): 114–35.

Gray, B. and Yan, A. (1992) 'A negotiations model of joint venture formation, structure and performance: implications for global management', *Advances in International Comparative Management* 7: 41–75.

Guest, D. (1990) 'Human resources and the American dream', *Journal of Management Studies* 27: 377–97.

Haire, M., Ghiselli, M. M. and Porter, L. W. (1966) *Managerial Thinking: An International Study*, New York: John Wiley.

Hall, R. I. (1976) 'A system pathology of organization: the rise and fall of the old Saturday Evening Post', *Administrative Science Quarterly* 21: 185–211.

Hamel, G., Doz, Y. L. and Prahalad, C. K. (1989) 'Collaborate with your competitors and win', *Harvard Business Review* 67(1): 133–9.

Hampden-Turner, C. and Trompenaars, A. (1993) *The Seven Cultures of Capitalism*, New York: Doubleday.

Haspeslagh, P. C. and Jemison, D. B. (1991) *Managing Acquisitions: Creating Value Through Corporate Renewal*, New York: Free Press.

Heller, F., Drenth, P., Koopman, P. and Rus, V. (1988) *Decisions in Organizations: A Three Country Comparative Study*, London: Sage.

Hennart, J.-F., Barkema, H., Bell, J., Benito, G. R. G., Larimo, J., Pedersen, T. and Zeng, M. (1997) 'The impact of national origin on the survival of foreign affiliates: a comparative study of North European and Japanese investors in the United States', in *Innovation and International Business: Proceedings of the Annual Meeting of the European International Business Academy*, vol. 1: 342–65, Stockholm: Institute of International Business.

Hickson, D. J., Butler, R. J., Cray, D., Mallory, G. R. and Wilson, D. C. (1986) *Top Decisions: Strategic Decision making in Organizations*, Oxford: Blackwell.

Hickson, D. J., Hinings, C. R., McMillan, C. J. and Schwitter, J. P. (1974) 'The culture-free context of organizational structure: a tri-national comparison', *Sociology* 8: 59–80.

Hickson, D. J. and McMillan, C. J. (eds) (1981) *Organization and Nation: The Aston Programme IV*, Farnborough: Gower.

Hickson, D. J., McMillan, C. J., Azumi, K. and Horvath, D. (1979) 'Grounds for comparative organization theory: quicksands or hard core?', in C. J. Lammers and D. J. Hickson (eds) *Organizations Alike and Unlike*, London: Routledge & Kegan Paul.

Hickson, D. J. and Pugh, D. S. (1995) *Management Worldwide: The Impact of Societal Culture on Organizations around the Globe*, London: Penguin.

Hilton, G. (1972) 'Causal inference analysis: a seductive process', *Administrative Science Quarterly* 17: 44–54.

Hoffman, R. C. and Hegarty, W. H. (1989) 'Convergence or divergence of strategic decision processes among 10 nations', in C. A. B. Osigweh, Yg. (ed.) *Organizational Science Abroad: Constraints and Perspectives*, New York: Plenum.

Hofstede, G. (1980a) *Culture's Consequences: International Differences in Work-related Values*, Beverly Hills, CA: Sage.

—— (1980b) 'Motivation, leadership and organization: do American theories apply abroad?', *Organizational Dynamics* 9(1): 42–63.

—— (1985) 'The interaction between national and organizational value systems', *Journal of Management Studies* 22: 347–57.

—— (1991) *Culture and Organizations: Software of the Mind*, London: McGraw-Hill.

Hofstede, G and Bond, M. H. (1988) 'The Confucius connection: from cultural roots to economic growth', *Organizational Dynamics* 16(4): 5–21.

Hofstede, G., Bond, M. H. and Luk, C.L. (1993) 'Individual perceptions of organizational cultures: a methodological treatise on levels of analysis', *Organization Studies* 14: 483–503.

Hofstede, G., Neuijen, B., Ohayv, D. D. and Sanders, G. (1990) 'Measuring organizational cultures: a qualitative and quantitative study across twenty cases', *Administrative Science Quarterly* 35: 286–316.

Hogarth, R. M. (1987) *Judgement and Choice: the Psychology of Decision*, 2nd edn., Chichester: Wiley.

Howell, J. P., Bowen, D. E., Dorfman, P. W., Kerr, S. and Podsakoff, P. M. (1990) 'Substitutes for leadership: effective alternatives to ineffective leadership', *Organizational Dynamics* 19(1): 21–38.

Huczynski, A. A. (1993) *Management Gurus*, London: Routledge.

Huff, A. S. (1990) 'Mapping strategic thought', in A. S. Huff (ed.) *Mapping Strategic Thought*, Chichester: Wiley.

Hunt, J. W. (1981) 'Applying American behavioral science: some cross-cultural problems', *Organizational Dynamics* 10(1): 55–62.

Hunter, J. E., Schmidt, F. L. and Jackson, G. B. (1982) *Meta-Analysis: Cumulating Research Findings Across Studies*, Beverly Hills, CA: Sage.

Inkson, J. H. K., Schwitter, J. P., Pheysey, D. C. and Hickson, D. J. (1981) 'A comparison of organization structure and managerial roles: Ohio, USA and the Midlands, England', in D. J. Hickson and C. J. McMillan (eds) *Organization and Nation: The Aston Programme IV*, Farnborough: Gower.

James, L. R., Joyce, W. F. and Slocum, J. W., Jr (1988) 'Organizations do not cognize', *Academy of Management Review* 13: 129–32.

Jamieson, I. (1980) *Capitalism and Culture: A Comparative Analysis of British and American Manufacturing Organizations*, Farnborough: Gower.

Johanson, J. and Vahlne, J.-E. (1977) 'The internationalization process of the firm: a model of knowledge development and increasing foreign market commitments', *Journal of International Business Studies* 8(1): 23–32.

—— (1990) 'The mechanism of internationalisation', *International Marketing Review* 7: 11–24.

Kedia, B. L. and Bhagat, R. S. (1988) 'Cultural constraints on transfer of technology across nations: implications for research in international and comparative management', *Academy of Management Review* 13: 559–71.

Kelley, L., Whatley, A. and Worthley, R. (1987) 'Assessing the effects of culture on managerial attitudes: a three-culture test', *Journal of International Business Studies* 18: 17–31.

Kerr, C., Dunlop, J. T, Harbison, F. H. and Myers, C. A. (1960) *Industrialism and Industrial Man*, Cambridge, MA: Harvard University Press.

Kets de Vries, M. F. R. and Mead, C. (1992) 'The development of the global leader within the multinational corporation', in V. Pucik, N. M. Tichy and C. K. Barnett (eds) *Globalizing Management: Creating and Leading the Competitive Organization*, New York: Wiley.

Khadra, B. (1990) 'The prophetic-caliphal model of leadership: an empirical study', *International Studies of Management and Organization* 20: 37–51.

Killing, J. P. (1983) *Strategies for Joint Venture Success*, New York: Praeger.

Kim, K. I., Park, H.-J. and Suzuki, N. (1990) 'Reward allocations in the United States, Japan and Korea: a comparison of individualistic and collectivistic cultures', *Academy of Management Journal* 33: 188–98.

Kipnis, D., Schmidt, S. M. and Wilkinson, I. (1980) 'Intraorgnizational influence tactics: explorations in getting one's way', *Journal of Applied Psychology* 65: 440–52.

Kirkpatrick, S. A. and Locke, E. A. (1991) 'Leadership: do traits really matter?', *Academy of Management Executive* 5(2): 48–60.

Kobrin, S. J. (1994) 'Is there a relationship between a geocentric mind-set and multinational strategy?', *Journal of International Business Studies* 25: 493–511.

Kogut, B. and Singh, H. (1988) 'The effect of national culture on the choice of entry mode', *Journal of International Business Studies* 19: 411–32.

Kozan, M. K. (1993) 'Cultural and industrialization level influences on leadership attitudes for Turkish managers', *International Studies of Management and Organization* 23(3): 7–17.

Kraut, A. I. (1975) 'Some recent advances in cross-national research', *Academy of Management Journal* 18: 538–49.

Kroeber, A. L. and Kluckhohn, C. (1952) *Culture: A Critical Review of Concepts and Definitions*, Cambridge, MA: Peabody Museum.

Lammers, C. J. and Hickson, D. J. (eds) (1979a) *Organizations Alike and Unlike*, London: Routledge & Kegan Paul.

—— (1979b) 'Are organizations culture-bound?', in C. J. Lammers and D. J. Hickson (eds) *Organizations Alike and Unlike*, London: Routledge & Kegan Paul.

Langfield-Smith, K. (1992) 'Exploring the need for a shared cognitive map', *Journal of Management Studies* 29: 349–68.

Langfield-Smith, K. and Wirth, A. (1992) 'Measuring differences between cognitive maps', *Journal of the Operational Research Society* 43: 1135–50.

Laukkanen, M. (1994) 'Comparative cause mapping of organizational cognitions', *Organization Science* 5: 322–43.

Lawrence, P. (1991) 'The personnel function: an Anglo-German comparison', in C. Brewster and S. Tyson (eds) *International Comparisons in Human Resource Management*, London: Pitman.

Lawrence, P. R.. and Lorsch, J. W. (1967) *Organization and Environment*, Homewood, IL: Irwin.

Lawrence, P. R. and Vlachoutsicos, C. A. (1990) 'Managerial patterns: differences and commonalities', in P. R. Lawence and C. A. Vlachoutsicos (eds) *Behind the Factory Walls: Decision Making in Soviet and U.S. Enterprises*, Boston, MA: Harvard Business School.

Legge, K. (1989) 'Human resource management: a critical review', in J. Storey (ed.) *New Perspectives on Human Resource Management*, London: Routledge.

Levitt, T. (1983) 'The globalization of markets', *Harvard Business Review* 61(3): 92–102.

Li, J. (1995) 'Foreign entry and survival: effects of strategic choice on performance in international markets', *Strategic Management Journal* 16: 333–51.

Li, J. and Guisinger, S. (1992) 'The globalization of service multinationals in the "Triad" Nations: Japan, Europe and North America', *Journal of International Business Studies* 23: 675–96.

Li, P. P. (1993) 'How national context influences corporate strategy: a comparison of South Korea and Taiwan', *Advances in International Comparative Management* 8: 55–78.

Lincoln, J., Hanada, M. and McBride, K. (1986) 'Organizational structures in Japanese and U.S. Manufacturing', *Administrative Science Quarterly* 31: 338–64.

Lincoln, Y. S. and Guba, E. G. (1985) *Naturalistic Inquiry*, Beverly Hills, CA: Sage.

Loree, D. W. and Guisinger, S. E. (1995) 'Policy and non-policy determinants of U.S. equity foreign direct investment', *Journal of International Business Studies* 26: 281–99.

Mabey, C. and Mallory, G. R. (1995) 'Structure and culture change in two UK organizations: a comparison of assumptions, approaches and outcomes', *Human Resource Management Journal* 5(2): 28–45.

MacLean, N. (1992) *Young Men and Fire*, Chicago, IL: University of Chicago Press.

Mallory, G. R., Butler, R. J., Cray, D., Hickson, D. J. and Wilson, D. C. (1983) 'Implanted decision making: American owned firms in Britain', *Journal of Management Studies* 20: 191–211.

Mallory, G. R. and Cray, D. (1982) 'Tactical and strategic decision making', paper delivered at the American Sociological Association, San Francisco, CA, September.

Martin, J. and Meyerson, D. (1988) 'Organizational cultures and the denial, channelling and acknowledgement of ambiguity', in L. R. Pondy, R. J. Boland, Jr, and H. Thomas (eds) *Managing Ambiguity and Change*, New York: Wiley.

Martinez, Z. L. and Ricks, D. A. (1989) 'Multinational parent companies' influence over human resource decisions of affiliates: U.S. firms in Mexico', *Journal of International Business Studies* 20: 465–87.

Maurice, M. (1979) 'For a study of "the societal effect": universality and specificity in organization research', in C. L. Lammers and D. J. Hickson (eds) *Organizations Alike and Unlike*, London: Routledge & Kegan Paul.

Meek, V. L. (1988) 'Organizational culture: origins and weaknesses', *Organization Studies* 9: 453–73.

Meschi, P.-X. and Roger, A. (1994) 'Cultural context and social effectiveness in international joint ventures', *Management International Review* 34(3): 197–215.

Meyerson, D. and Martin, J. (1987) 'Cultural change: an integration of three different views', *Journal of Management Studies* 24: 623–47.

Miller, E. J. (1975) 'Socio-technical systems in weaving, 1953–1970: a follow-up study', *Human Relations* 28: 349–86.

Miller, G. A. (1987) 'Meta-analysis and the culture-free hypothesis', *Organization Studies* 8: 309–25.

Mintzberg, H., Raisinghani, D. and Theoret, A. (1976) 'The structure of "unstructured" decision processes', *Administrative Science Quarterly* 21: 246–75.

Morosini, P. and Singh, H. (1994) 'Post-cross-border acquisitions: implementing "national culture-compatible" strategies to improve performance', *European Management Journal* 12: 390–400.

Morris, T. and Pavett, C. M. (1992) 'Management style and productivity in two cultures', *Journal of International Business Studies* 23: 169–79.

Ouchi, W. G. (1981) *Theory Z: how American business can meet the Japanese challenge*, Reading, MA: Addison-Wesley.

Parkhe, A. (1993) "Messy" research, methodological predispositions, and theory development in international joint ventures', *Academy of Management Review* 18: 227–68.

Peters, T. J. and Waterman, R. H., Jr (1982) *In Search of Excellence: Lessons from America's Best-run Companies*, New York: Harper.

Peterson, M. F., Brannen, M. Y., and Smith, P. B. (1994) 'Japanese and United States leadership: issues in current research', *Advances in International and Comparative Management* 9: 57–82.

Pettigrew, A. M. (1973) *The Politics of Organisational Decision-making*, London: Tavistock.

Pieper, R. (1990) 'Introduction', in R. Pieper (ed.) *Human Resource Management: An International Comparison*, Berlin: de Gruyter.

Pontusson, J. (1990) 'The politics of new technology and job redesign: a comparison of Volvo and British Leyland', *Economic and Industrial Democracy* 11: 311–36.

Poole, M. (1990) 'Human resource management in an international perspective', *International Journal of Human Resource Management* 1: 1–15.

Porter, M. E. (1986) 'Changing patterns in international competition', *California Management Review* 28(2): 9–40.

—— (1990) *The Competitive Advantage of Nations*, New York: The Free Press.

Pugh, D. S. (1989) 'The convergence of international organizational behaviour', Open University School of Management working paper.

Pugh, D. S., Clark, T. A. R. and Mallory, G. R. (1996) 'Organization, structure and structural change in European manufacturing organizations', in P. J. D. Drenth, P. L. Koopman and B. Wilpert (eds) *Organizational Decision making under Different Economic and Political Conditions*, Amsterdam: North-Holland Press.

Pugh, D. S. and Hickson, D. J. (1976) *Organizational Structure in Its Context: The Aston Programme I*, Farnborough: Saxon House.

—— (1996) 'Organizational convergence', in M. Warner (ed.) *International Encyclopedia of Business and Management*, vol. 4, London: Routledge.

Pugh, D. S., Hickson, D. J., and Hinings, C. R. (1969a) 'An empirical taxonomy of structures of work organizations', *Administrative Science Quarterly* 14: 115–26.

Pugh, D. S., Hickson, D. J., Hinings, C. R. and Turner, C. (1969b) 'The context of organization structures', *Administrative Science Quarterly* 14: 91–114.

Pugh, D. S. and Hinings, C. R. (eds) (1976) *Organizational Structure Extensions and Replications: The Aston Programme II*, Farnborough: Saxon House.

Punnett, B. J. and Withane, S. (1990) 'Hofstede's value survey module: to embrace or abandon?', *Advances in International Comparative Management* 5: 69–89.

Purves, B. (1991) *Barefoot in the Boardroom: Venture and Misadventure in the People's Republic of China*, Sydney: Allen & Unwin.

Rajan, M. N. and Graham, J. L. (1991) 'Nobody's grandfather was a merchant: understanding the Soviet commercial negotiation process and style', *California Management Review* 33(3): 40–57.

Ralston, D. A., Gustafson, D. J., Cheung, F. M and Terpstra, R. H. (1993) 'Differences in managerial values: a study of U.S., Hong Kong and PRC managers', *Journal of International Business Studies* 24: 249–75.

Rao, A. and Schmidt, S. M. (1995) 'Intercultural influence: an Asian perspective', *Advances in International Comparative Management* 10: 79–98.

Redding, S. G. (1994) 'Comparative management theory: jungle, zoo or fossil bed?', *Organization Studies* 15: 323–59.

Rice, A. K. (1958) *Productivity and Social Organization: the Ahmedebad Experiment*, London: Tavistock.

Roberts, K. H. (1970) 'On looking at an elephant: an evaluation of cross-cultural research related to organizations', *Psychological Bulletin* 4: 327–50.

Roberts, K. H. and Boyacigiller, N. A. (1984) 'Cross-national organizational research: the grasp of the blind men', *Research in Organizational Behaviour* 6: 423–75.

Robinson, R. V. (1983) 'Geert Hofstede: *Culture's Consequences*: international differences in work-related values', *Work and Occupations* 10: 110–15.

Rodrigues, C. A. (1990) 'The situation and national culture as contingencies for leadership behaviour: two conceptual models', *Advances in International Comparative Management* 5: 51–68.

Rosenzweig, P. M. and Nohria, N. (1994) 'Influences on human resource management practices in multinational corporations', *Journal of International Business Studies* 25: 229–51.

Salaman, G. (1978) 'Towards a sociology of organisational structure', *The Sociological Review* 26: 519–54.

Schein, E. (1983) 'The role of the founder in creating organizational culture', *Organizational Dynamics* 12(1): 13–28.

Schendel, D. E. and Hofer, C. W. (1979) 'Introduction', in D. E. Schendel and C. W. Hofer (eds) *Strategic Management: A New View of Business Policy and Planning*, Boston, MA: Little Brown.

Schermerhorn, J. R. Jr, and Nyaw, M.-K. (1990) 'Managerial leadership in Chinese industrial enterprises', *International Studies of Management and Organization* 20: 9–21.

Schmidt S. M and Yeh, R.-S. (1992) 'The structure of leader influence: a cross-national comparison', *Journal of Cross-cultural Psychology* 23: 251–64.

Schneider, S. C. (1989) 'Strategy formulation: the impact of national culture', *Organization Studies* 10: 149–68.

Schneider, S. C. and Angelmar, R. (1993) 'Cognition in organizational analysis: who's minding the store?', *Organization Studies* 14: 347–74.

Schuler, R. S., Dowling, P. J. and De Cieri, H. (1993) 'An integrative framework of strategic international human resource management', *Journal of Management* 19: 419–59.

Scott, B. R. (1973) 'The industrial state: old myths and new realities', *Harvard Business Review* 51(2): 133–48.

Scott, W. R., Dornbusch, S. M. and Utande, E. A. (1979) 'Organizational control: a comparison of authority systems in US and Nigerian organizations', in C. J. Lammers and D. J. Hickson (eds) *Organizations Alike and Unlike*, London: Routledge & Kegan Paul.

Servain-Schreiber, J.-J. (1968) *The American Challenge*, New York: Avon.

Shackleton, V. J. and Ali, A. H. (1990) 'Work-related values of managers: a test of the Hofstede model', *Journal of Cross-cultural Psychology* 21: 109–18.

Shane, S. A. (1993) 'The effect of cultural differences in perceptions of transactions costs on national differences in the preference for international joint ventures', *Asia Pacific Journal of Management* 10: 57–69.

Shenkar, O. and Zeira, Y. (1992) 'Role conflict and role ambiguity of chief executive officers in international joint ventures', *Journal of International Business Studies* 23: 55–75.

Shore, B. and Venkatachalam, A. R. (1995) 'The role of national culture in systems analysis and design', *Journal of Global Information Management* 3(3): 5–14.

Simon, H. A. (1957) *Administrative Behavior*, 2nd edn, New York: Macmillan.

Smith. P. B. (1992) 'Organizational behaviour and national cultures', *British Journal of Management* 3: 39–51.

Sondergaard, M. (1994) 'Research note: Hofstede's *Consequences*: a study of reviews, citations and replications', *Organization Studies* 15: 447–56.

Sorge, A. (1983) 'Review of "Culture's Consequences: International Differences in Work-related Values"', *Administrative Science Quarterly* 28: 625–9.

—— (1991) 'Strategic fit and the societal effect: interpreting cross-national comparisons of technology, organization and human resources', *Organization Studies* 12: 161–90.

Starbuck, W. H. (1981) 'A trip to view the elephants and rattlesnakes in the garden of Aston', in A. H. Van de Ven and W. F. Joyce (eds) *Perspectives on Organizational Design and Behavior*, New York: Wiley.

Staw, B. M. (1981) 'The escalation of commitment to a course of action', *Academy of Management Review* 6: 577–87.

Steers, R. M., Bischoff, S. J. and Higgins, L. H. (1992) 'Cross-cultural management research: the fish and the fisherman', *Journal of Management Inquiry* 1: 321–30.

Stopford, J. M. and Wells, L. T., Jr (1972) *Managing the Multinational Enterprise*, New York: Basic Books.

Storey, J. (1992) *Developments in the Management of Human Resources: An Analytical Review*: Oxford: Blackwell.

Sutton, R. I. and Staw, B. M. (1995) 'What theory is *not*', *Administrative Science Quarterly* 40: 371–84.

Tayeb, M. (1988) *Organizations and National Culture: A Comparative Analysis*, London: Sage.

Taylor, F. W. (1947) *Scientific Management*, New York: Harper & Row.

Taylor, S., Beechler, S. and Napier, N. (1996) 'Toward an integrative model of strategic international human resource management', *Academy of Management Review* 21: 959–85.

Teagarden, M. B. and von Glinow, M. A. (1990) 'Contextual determinants of HRM effectiveness in cooperative alliances: Mexican evidence', *Management International Review* 30: 23–36, special issue.

Thomas, J. B., Clark, S. M. and Gioia, D. A. (1993) 'Strategic sensemaking and organization performance: linkages among scanning, interpretation, action and outcomes', *Academy of Management Journal* 36: 239–70.

Thompson, J. D. (1967) *Organizations in Action*, New York: McGraw-Hill.

Triandis, H. C. (1982) 'Review of *Culture's Consequences: International Differences in Work-related Values*', *Human Organization* 41: 86–90.

—— (1994) 'Cross-cultural industrial and organizational psychology', in H. C. Triandis, M. D. Dunnette and L. M. Hough (eds) *Handbook of Industrial and Organizational Psychology*, 2nd edn, vol. 4, Palo Alto, CA: Consulting Psychologists Press.

Tricker, R. I (1994) 'The board's role in strategy formulation: some cross-cultural comparisons', *Futures* 26: 403–15.

Trist, E. L. and Bamforth, K. W. (1951) 'Some social and psychological consequences of the longwall method of coal getting', *Human Relations* 4: 3–38.

Trist, E. L., Higgin, G. W., Murray H. and Pollock, A. B. (1963) *Organizational Choice*, London: Tavistock.

Trompenaars, F. (1993), *Riding the Waves of Culture: Understanding Cultural Diversity in Business*, London: Nicholas Brearley.

Tse, D. K., Lee, K., Vertinsky, I. and Wehrung, D. A. (1988) 'Does culture matter? A cross-cultural study of executives' choice, decisiveness and risk adjustment in international marketing', *Journal of Marketing* 52(4): 81–95.

Tung, R. L. (1988) 'Toward a conceptual paradigm of international business negotiations', *Advances in International Comparative Management* 3: 203–19.

Turner, B. A. (1986) 'Sociological aspects of organizational symbolism', *Organization Studies* 7: 101–15.

Turpin, D. (1993) 'Strategic alliances with Japanese firms: myths and realities', *Long Range Planning* 26(4): 11–15.

Tversky, A. and Kahnemen, D. (1974) 'Judgement under uncertainty: heuristics and biases', *Science* 185: 1124–31.

Vance, C. M., McLaine, S. R., Boje, D. M. and Stage, H. D. (1992) 'An examination of the transferability of traditional performance appraisal principles across cultural boundaries', *Management International Review* 32: 313–26.

Walsh, J. P., Henderson, C. M. and Deighton, J. A. (1988) 'Negotiated belief structures and decision performance: an empirical investigation', *Organizational Behavior and Human Decision Processes* 42: 194–216.

Weick, K. E. (1979) *The Social Psychology of Organizing*, 2nd edn, Reading, MA: Addison-Wesley.

—— (1988) 'Enacted sensemaking in crisis situations', *Journal of Management Studies* 25: 305–17.

—— (1990) 'Introduction: cartographic myths in organizations', in A. S. Huff (ed.) *Mapping Strategic Thought*, Chichester: Wiley.

—— (1993) 'The collapse of sensemaking in organizations: the Mann Gulch disaster', *Administrative Science Quarterly* 38: 628–52.

—— (1995) *Sensemaking in Organizations*, Thousand Oaks, CA: Sage.

Weiss, S. E. (1994) 'Negotiating with "Romans" – part 1', *Sloan Management Review* 35(2): 51–61.

Wild, R. (1975) *Work Organization*, London: Wiley.

Wilms, W. W., Hardcastle, A. J. and Zell, D. M. (1994) 'Cultural transformation at NUMMI', *Sloan Management Review* 36(1): 99–113.

Wong-Rieger, D. and Rieger, F. (1989) 'The influence of societal culture on corporate culture, business strategy, and performance in the international airline industry', in C. A. B. Osigweh, Yg. (ed.) *Organizational Science Abroad: Constraints and Perspectives*, New York: Plenum.

Woodward, J. (1965) *Industrial Organization: Theory and Practice*, London: Oxford University Press.

Zhu, C. J., Dowling, P. J. and Holland, P. J. (1996) 'Performance appraisal in Australia and China: an analysis of best practices', Department of Business Management working paper 4-96, Monash University, Melbourne.

Name Index

Abrahmson, E. 110
Ackerman, F. 161
Adler, N.J. 2, 4, 10, 11, 13, 17, 19, 21, 23, 36, 90, 111, 122, 148, 161
Aiken, M. 42
Al-Aiban 33, 34, 36
Aldrich H.E. 47
Ali, A.H. 55, 56
Ali, A.J. 71, 74
Allen, T.J. 1
Alvesson, M. 101, 103, 141, 156, 157, 161
Angelmar, R. 93, 105, 112
Argyris, C. 154
Axelsson, R. 49, 55, 56, 69, 74, 81, 88
Azumi, K. 25, 40, 43–44, 60

Bacharach, S.B. 42
Baird, I.S. 76, 80
Bamforth, K.W. 130
Barkema, H.G. 73, 74
Barrett, C.V. 36
Bartlett, C.A. 5, 66, 67
Bass, B.M. 36
Beaumont, P.B. 116, 117
Beck, B.E.F. 103
Bedard, R. 30
Beechler, S. 28, 121, 122, 137
Beer, M. 116, 117
Bell, J.H. 73, 74
Benito, G.R.G. 73
Berggren, C. 133, 134, 136

Bhagat, R.S. 84, 85, 88
Binkhorst, D. 93
Bischoff, S.J. 29
Black, J.S. 125, 136
Blankenburg, E. 46
Blau, P.M. 24
Boje, D.M. 120, 123
Bond, M.H. 8, 50, 60, 76, 103, 110
Bougon, M. 93
Bowen, D.E. 114
Boyacigiller, N.A. 2, 4, 13, 14, 19, 21, 23, 36
Brannen, M.Y. 32
Braye, C.E. 2
Brewster, C. 118, 137
Brown, A. 30, 69, 74
Brown, L.T. 77
Bruner, J. 92, 156, 157
Buckley, P.J. 75
Butler, R.J. 46, 81

Calori, R. 83, 84, 108–111, 112, 129, 146, 148
Campbell, D.T. 18
Casson, M. 75
Caunch, C.L. 2
Chandler, A.D. 40, 63
Chanlat, A. 30
Channon, D. 40
Chatterjee, S. 82, 84
Cheung, F.M. 125, 129
Child, J. 41, 42, 43–44, 46, 47, 48, 49, 55, 58

Clark, P. 72
Clark, S.M. 4
Clark, T.A.R. 55, 56, 66, 116, 117, 118, 119, 137
Contractor, F.J. 76
Cray, D. 6, 43, 46, 49, 55, 56, 69, 74, 81, 88, 94
Cropper, S. 161
Cullen, J.B. 78, 88
Czarniawska-Joerges, B. 156

Datta, D.K. 82, 84
Deal, T.E. 102
De Cieri, H. 122
Deighton, J.A. 93, 112
Devanna, M.A. 116
Donaldson, L. 44–46, 47
Donnellon, A. 151, 156
Dorfman, P.W. 53, 114
Dornbusch, S.M. 42
Douglas, S.P. 65–66
Dowling, P.J. 121, 122, 123
Doz, Y.L. 66
Drenth, P.J.D. 30, 69, 74
Drew, P. 94, 156
Dubin, R. 31–32, 41
Dubinsky, A.J. 34–35, 36
Dunlop, J.T. 39
Dunning, J.H. 48
Dunphy, D.C. 30
Dutton, J.E. 110
Dyas, G.P. 40

Earley, P.C. 20
Eden, C. 95, 161
England, G.W. 60
Erramilli, M.K. 72, 74, 88

Fant, L. 161
Fayol, H. 39
Fiol, C.M. 95
Fletcher, K.E. 95
Fombrun, C.J. 116

Gagliardi, P. 104
Galbraith, J.R. 40, 64
Gallie, D. 48

Ganitsky, J. 76
Gardner, H. 92, 157
Geertz, C. 156
Ghadar, F. 122
Ghertman, M. 81
Ghiselli, M.M. 127
Ghoshal, S. 2, 5, 21, 48, 66, 67
Gibson, C.B. 127, 129, 137
Gilbert, G.N. 156, 161
Gioia, D.A. 4, 97, 151, 153, 156, 161
Glick, W.H. 104
Godkin, L. 2
Goodstein, L.D. 52
Graham, J.L. 10, 11, 17, 21, 145, 148, 161
Grant, R.M. 67
Gray, B. 75
Guba, E.G. 91
Guest, D. 115
Guisinger, S.E. 72
Gustafson, D.J. 125, 129

Haines, G.H. 94
Haire, M. 127
Hall, R.I. 95
Hamel, G. 66
Hampden-Turner, C. 25, 26, 32, 60
Hanada, M. 2, 40, 61
Harbison, F.H. 39
Hardcastle, A.J. 133
Haspeslagh, P.C. 81
Hauptman, O. 1
Hegarty, W.H. 72
Heller, F. 30, 69, 74
Henderson, C.M. 93, 112
Hennart, J.-F. 73
Heritage. J. 94, 156
Hickson, D.J. 2, 18, 24, 25, 28, 39, 40, 41, 42–44, 46, 47, 58, 60, 61, 81, 139–140
Higgin, G.W. 115
Higgins, L.H. 29
Hilton, G. 47
Hinings, C.R. 18, 24, 41
Hofer, C.W. 43
Hoffman, R.C. 72

Hofstede, G. 2, 3, 8, 9, 21, 25, 26, 28, 35, 49–58, 60, 76, 81, 85, 87, 89, 91, 102, 103, 109, 110, 112, 115, 124, 139–143, 146
Hogarth, R.M. 94
Holland, P.J. 121, 123
Horvath, D. 25, 40, 43–44, 60
Howell, J.P. 53, 114
Huczynski, A.A. 130
Huff, A.S. 94, 95, 148, 161
Hunt, J.W. 52–53
Hunter, J.E. 44

Inkson, J.H.K. 41, 42

Jackson, G.B. 44
James, L.R. 104
Jamieson, I. 30, 46
Jemison, D.B. 81
Joerges, B. 156
Johanson, J. 66, 67
Johnson, G. 108–111, 112, 129, 146, 148
Johnson, J.L. 78, 88
Jolson, M.A. 34–35, 36
Joyce, W.F. 104

Kahnemen, D. 93
Kedia, B.L. 84, 85, 88
Kelley, L. 34, 36, 60
Kennedy, A.A. 102
Kerr, C. 39
Kerr, S. 114
Kets de Vries, M.F.R. 28
Khadra, B. 124
Kieser, A. 41, 42
Killing, J.P. 66
Kim, K.I. 34–35, 36
Kipnis, B. 126
Kirkpatrick, S.A. 114
Kluckhohn, C. 15
Kobrin, S.J. 67
Kogut, B. 71, 72, 74, 86, 154
Koopman, P.L. 30, 69, 74
Kotabe, M. 34–35, 36
Kozan, M.K. 127, 129
Kraut, A.I 16

Kroeber, A.L. 15

Lammers, C.J. 47, 58, 61
Langfield-Smith, K. 93, 104, 112
Larimo, J. 73
Laukkanen, M. 94, 105, 110, 112
Laurence, P.R. 116, 117
Lawrence, P. 119, 123
Lawrence, P.R. 24, 41, 70
Lee, K. 70, 74
Legge, K. 114
Levitt, T. 64–65, 67
Li, J. 72, 73
Li, P.P. 72
Lim, C.U. 34–35, 36
Lincoln, J. 2, 40, 61
Lincoln, Y.S. 91
Locke, E.A. 114
Loree, D.W. 72
Lorsch, J.W. 24, 41
Lubatkin, M.H. 82, 83, 84
Luk, C.L. 60, 103
Lyles, M.A. 76, 80

Mabey, C. 132, 134
MacLean, N. 153
McBride, K. 2, 40, 61
McLaine, S.R. 120, 123
McMillan, C.J. 18, 24, 25, 40, 41, 42–44, 46, 47, 60
Mallory, G.R. 43, 46, 49, 55, 56, 66, 69, 74, 81, 88, 116, 117, 118, 132, 134, 137
Martin, J. 103, 105
Martinez, Z.L. 122, 123
Maurice, M. 43–44, 47
Mead, C. 28
Meek, V.L. 101
Meschi, P.-X. 79, 80
Meyerson, D. 103, 105
Miller, E.J. 131
Miller, G.A. 45
Mills, D.Q. 116, 117
Mintzberg, H. 155
Moore, L.F. 103
Morosini, P. 82, 84, 88
Morris, T. 125, 128, 129

Mueller, F. 72
Mulkay, M. 156, 161
Murray, H. 115
Myers, C.A. 39

Napier, N. 28, 121, 122, 137
Nathanson, D.A. 40, 64
Neuijen, B. 8, 91, 102, 103, 109, 112, 142, 143, 146
Nohria, N. 122
Nyaw, M.-K. 126

Odar, M. 30, 69, 74
Ohayv, D.D. 8, 91, 102, 103, 109, 112, 142, 143, 146
Ouchi, W.G. 101, 115, 116

Park, H.-J. 34–35, 36
Parkhe, A. 80
Pavett, C.M. 125, 128, 129
Pearce, J.L. 33, 34, 36
Pedersen, T. 73
Pennings, J.M. 73, 74
Peters, T.J. 102, 115, 116
Peterson, M.F. 32
Pettigrew, A.M. 81
Pheysey, D.C. 41, 42
Pieper, R. 118
Podsakoff, P.M. 114
Pollock, A.B. 115
Pontusson, J. 132, 137
Poole, M. 117
Poole, P.P. 161
Porter, L.W. 125, 127, 136
Porter, M.E. 48, 64, 67
Prahalad, C.K. 66
Pugh, D.S. 2, 24, 28, 39, 41, 49, 55, 56, 119, 139–140
Punnett, B.J. 55–57, 61
Purves, B. 126

Raisinghani, D. 155
Rajan, M.N. 148
Ralston, D.A. 125, 129
Rao, A. 3
Redding, S.G. 2, 3, 4, 13, 20, 21, 23, 36, 37, 49, 140

Rice, A.K. 115, 130, 134
Ricks, D.A. 122, 123
Rieger, F. 101
Roberts, K.H. 14, 21, 23
Robinson, R.V. 53
Rodrigues, C.A. 128, 137
Roger, A. 79, 80
Rosenzweig, P.M. 122
Rugman, A.M. 77
Rus, V. 30, 69, 74

Sakano, T. 78, 88
Salaman, G. 47, 58
Sanders, G. 8, 91, 102, 103, 109, 112, 142, 143, 146
Sarnin, P. 108–111, 112, 129, 146, 148
Schein E. 104
Schendel, D.E. 43
Schermerhorn, J.R. 126
Schmidt, F.L. 44
Schmidt, S.M. 3, 126, 129
Schneider, S.C. 68, 73, 88, 93, 105, 112
Schoenherr, R.A. 24
Schuler, R.S. 122
Schweiger, D.M. 82, 84
Schwitter, J.P. 18, 24, 41, 42
Scott, B.R. 40
Scott, W.R. 42
Servain-Schreiber, J.-J. 30, 32
Shackleton, V.J. 55, 56
Shane, S.A. 76, 80, 88
Shenkar, O. 77, 80, 86, 88
Shore, B. 7
Simon, H.A. 92
Sims, H.P. 151, 156
Singh, H. 20, 71, 72, 74, 82, 84, 86, 88, 154
Slocum, J.W. 104
Smith, P.B. 32, 90, 112
Sondergaard, M. 49, 54–55, 56, 140
Sorge, A. 48, 54
Spector, B. 116, 117
Stage, H.D. 120, 123
Stanley, J.C. 18
Starbuck, W.H. 47, 51

Staw, B.M. 93, 160
Steers, R.M. 29
Stopford,J.M. 64, 67
Storey, J. 116
Sutton, R.I. 160
Suzuki, N. 34–35, 36

Tayeb, M. 17, 21, 51, 54, 57
Taylor, F.W. 39
Taylor, S. 28, 121, 122, 137
Teagarden, M.B. 78–79, 80
Terpstra, R.H. 125, 129
Thanheiser, H.T. 40
Theoret, A. 155
Thomas, J.B. 4, 153
Thompson, J.D. 24
Tichy, N.M. 116
Triandis, H.C. 55, 61
Tricker, R.I. 70, 74
Trist, E.L. 115, 130
Trompenaars, A. 25, 26, 32, 60, 98, 103
Tse, D.K. 70, 74
Tung, R.L. 10, 11
Turner, B.A. 130
Turner, C. 24
Turpin, D. 78
Tversky, A. 93

Utande, E.A. 42

Vahlne, J.-E. 66, 67
Vance, C.M. 120, 123
Venkatachalam, A.R. 7
Verbeke, A. 77
Vertinsky, I. 70, 74

Very, P. 83, 84
Vlachoutsicos, C.A. 70
von Glinow, M.A. 78–79, 80

Walsh, J.P. 93, 112
Walton, E.J. 110
Walton, R.E. 116, 117
Waterman, R.H. 102, 115, 116
Watzke, G.E. 76
Weber, Y. 82, 84
Wehrung, D.A. 70, 74
Weick, K.E. 4, 48, 93, 96–97, 112, 153, 162
Weiss, S.E. 11
Wells, LT. 64, 67
Wharton, R. 76, 80
Whatley, A. 34, 36, 60
Wild, R. 132, 134
Wilkinson, I. 126
Wilms, W.W. 133
Wilson, D.C. 46, 49, 55, 56, 69, 74, 81, 88
Wind, Y. 65–66
Wirth, A. 93
Withane, S. 55–57, 61
Wong-Rieger, D. 101
Woodward, J. 40
Worthley, R. 34, 36, 60

Yan, A. 75
Yeh, R.-S. 126, 129

Zeira, Y, 77, 80, 86, 88
Zell, D.M. 133
Zeng, M. 73
Zhu, C.J. 121, 123

Subject Index

Acquisitions 80–83
Ambiguity 105
Approaches
   cognitive 92–112, 144–161
   culture-bound 24, 25, 49–58,
     59–60, 100
   culture-free 24, 25, 37–49, 59,
     100
   naive comparative 23–24, 25,
     29–37, 59, 100
   internationalist 26–28, 135, 150
Aston studies 38, 41, 43, 47
Australia 70–71, 121, 126, 127

Belgium 42
Boards of directors 70–71
British Leyland 131–132

Canada 55–56, 70
Centrism 2–3, 26–28
China 70, 121, 125
Cognition
   see also Approaches
   mapping 95–96, 108–110,
     147–150
   processes 93
   organizational 104–106
   structures 93, 151
   styles 93–94
Complexity 5–6
Convergence 39, 40–41, 64–65, 127
Cultural distance 71, 72–73, 79, 82,
   84–85, 87, 153

see also Culture
Culture
   see also Dimensions of culture
   and history 140
   and joint ventures 75–80
   change 51–52, 141
   definition 15–16
   fit 82
   industrial 9, 109, 146
   influence on strategy 64, 66–68,
     69–75
   integration 7–8
   levels 8–9, 98, 100–101, 145, 146
   national 98, 100–112, 144, 145
   organizational 100–112, 143
   professional 9, 109
   societal 143
   sociological view 141

Decision-making
   see also Strategy
   effects of culture 69–71, 73, 86
   process 70, 72–73, 81
   strategic 69, 81, 152–156
   style 71
Dimensions of culture
   and human resource management
     118
   benchmarks 141
   description 50–51
   criticism of 53–54, 142
   influence on strategy 72
   organizational 102

time 76, 110
use in research 55–57, 140
Discourse, *see* Language

Ethics 35
Ethnocentrism 17, 19
Expatriates 107, 122

Flexibility 150
Founders 9, 104
France 48, 82–83, 108

General Motors 132, 133
Germany 41, 104, 119–120
Globalization 64–65, 150

Hong Kong 70, 125
Human resource management
    see also Performance appraisal
    American origins 115–117
    definition 116
    European model 118–119
    in joint ventures 78
    international 115–123
    models 115–116, 118–119
    policies 121
    strategy 116
Hungary 79

India 130–131
Indonesia 120
Isuzu 132

Japan 30, 33–35, 70, 73, 78, 126, 151
Joint ventures 75–80

Kinship 99–100
Korea 34–35

Language
    and joint ventures 156–159
    discourse 156, 157, 158
    English 159
    in organizations 94
    in research 19, 110–111
Leadership
    and gender 127

context 126
criteria 150
effectiveness 125, 127
international 128–129, 150–152
situational 128
styles 125
Learning
    see also Strategy
    global 48
    organizational 5, 78
    second-order 154
Loyalty 106–107

Malawi 99
Malaysia 120
Mapping, maps
    see Cognition
Meta-analysis 42–46
Methodology
    comparisons 17
    data collection 109, 152
    generalizability 18, 44, 91
    problems 16–20, 142–143
    sampling 18–19, 35
Mexico 33–34, 78, 122, 125, 151
Mode of entry 71

Negotiation 9–12, 145, 147–150
Netherlands 69, 73, 119
Nigeria 41–42
Norway 127
Negotiation 9–11, 147–150
NUMMI 133–134

Organization
    design 7
    levels 136
    structure 40–42
Organizational culture, *see* Culture

Pakistan 55
Performance appraisal 120–121,
    156

Saudi Arabia 33
Scripts 97, 150–152
Sense-making 96, 99, 152–156

Sensitivity 155
Silence 145
South Korea 72
Spain 104
Strategy
  see also Decision-making
  agenda 147
  and structure 64
  content 72
  formulation 68–75
  implementation 73
  international 63–68
  learning 66–67
  marketing 64–66
  post-acquisition 82
  resources 67
  steps in formulating 68
  success 73, 87
Sudan 55
Sweden 30, 55, 69, 86, 119, 127

Taiwan 33–34, 72, 126
Technology 38, 40, 64, 65
  see also technology transfer
Technology transfer 83–85
Thailand 120
Theory
  cognitive 89–112, 143–161
  comparative 12–20, 23–26, 57–58
  contingency 38, 39–41
  retreat from 12–13, 142
Time 75–76, 81, 83, 108

Transaction costs 75, 77
Turkey 127

United Kingdom
  acquisitions 82–83
  cultural dimensions 55
  decision-making 69
  in comparison 30, 31–32, 41, 46,
    48
  leadership 126
  strategy 108
United States
  decision making 70
  direct investment 72
  in comparison 30, 31–32, 33–35,
    41
  investments in 71
  human resource management
    120, 122
  leadership 125, 127
  subsidiaries 46
Universalism 28, 38, 52, 118
USSR 70

Values 98, 102–103
Volvo 131–132

Work practices
  and culture 103
  transfer of 130–135

Yugoslavia 30, 69